Covering China

Media Studies Series

Robert Giles

Robert W. Snyder

Lisa DeLisle

editors

Covering China

Transaction Publishers

New Brunswick (U.S.A.) and London (U.K.)

Library of Congress Catalog Number: 00-068278
ISBN: 0–7658–0677–0
Printed in the United States of America

Library of Congress Cataloging-in-Publication Data

Covering China / Robert Giles, Robert W. Snyder, Lisa DeLisle, editors.
    p. cm.
  Originally published in the Media studies journal, Winter 1999.
  Includes bibliographical references and index.
  ISBN 0-7658-0677-0 (pbk. : alk. paper)
  1. China—Press coverage—United States. I. Giles, Robert H., 1993–
II. Snyder, Robert W. III. DeLisle, Lisa. IV. Media studies journal.

PN4888.C58 C68 2001
070.4'49951—dc21

                                                        00-068278

We gratefully acknowledge the editorial advice of Jonathan Sanders, Larry McGill, Rick Hornik, Kelly Haggart, Bette Bao Lord, Arnold Zeitlin and Jan Berris. We also thank Francine Abdow for her design modifications.

Contents

"Eighty years after the events of 1919, in a year of anniversaries when many of the debates closed off a decade ago are likely to be reopened with renewed vigor, the May 4th legacy should matter to everyone in the outside world who is interested in China's prospects for becoming a freer place," writes a historian.

"Overly romantic reporting about China in the 1930s and 1940s, a vital period in Chinese political history and Sino-American relations," a historian argues, "launched the roller coaster ride that has characterized the U.S.-China relationship and news media coverage ever since."

"We should have learned," writes a journalist who covered the fighting between the Nationalists and Communists, "that firepower in a civil war is not enough to prop up a regime that lacks popular support."

"During the years when China was closed to American reporters," a professor argues, "the dependency of American journalists on sources in Washington and their exclusion from Beijing in China reporting represented a journalistic deference to governmental politics."

A correspondent in Beijing surveys the Chinese media 10 years after Tiananmen: "The vibrance, diversity and enterprise of newspapers, magazines and television shows reflect growing pluralism and Beijing's inability to control it."

Part 2: Communicating

"For two generations of Americans, Buck invented China," writes an English professor. "Whatever the strengths or limits of her Asian images, she was a pioneer, introducing American readers to landscapes and people they had long ignored."

Ten years after the suppression of the democracy movement, a journalism professor notes that the events of 1989 shape American stories about China only intermittently: "The omission signals recognition that China has changed dramatically since 1989 as well as a growing convergence of editorial sentiment with foreign policy, or at least a grudging acceptance of the Clinton strategy of 'constructive engagement.'"

A reporter in Beijing compares coverage of the Clinton scandal in official Chinese media and tabloids and concludes, "If the way China looks at America is compared to the course of a great sailing ship, the vast populace on the decks remains forward-looking and even-keeled in the water, even if the government, perched way up on the masts, rocks back and forth, ordering zigzags due to changes in the wind."

"In modern China, the phrase 'guiding public opinion' is still heard and promulgated on the evening news and read in the papers," writes a Chinese journalist and dissident. "With 4,000 years of civilization, China has consistently produced leaders and advisors who seem especially artful in using language to their advantage, understanding all too well that cruel and brutal rule must be glossed over with a soft veneer."

"Eighteen months after Hong Kong was returned to Chinese rule, dire predictions of the demise of press freedom in this former British colony have not materialized," writes a Hong Kong correspondent. "Poised between China and the outside world, Hong Kong is still playing its traditional role of a bridge that enables the Chinese to understand themselves and the rest of the world to understand China."

"Freedom to think—not just to write what you want but to enable the mind to become an imaginative apparatus that can think what it wants—is very precious," says a journalism school dean with a long interest in China. "It is not something that comes easily in China or any totalitarian or communist society."

Part 3: Issues

"The cardinal sin committed by American news organizations in covering China is to portray it, always, in one overly simplistic frame," writes an author and former Beijing correspondent. "The American frames of China change dramatically from decade to decade, but the underlying behavior of the news organizations does not."

"The moorings that once secured the Chinese people's lives have come undone," writes a correspondent in Beijing. "For many women, that has been liberating. For others, it has been unsettling."

"In the ever more competitive fight for global capital, China will continue to earn its share only if it reforms its antiquated economic institutions and provides greater transparency," writes a correspondent in Hong Kong. "Journalists have to determine whether China is making progress, and that means penetrating the country's banks, companies and regulatory bodies."

"Sooner or later, the Yangzi dam is bound to re-emerge as one of the crucial issues of national debate," writes a media analyst. "This will create both an opportunity and a challenge for Western journalists."

"While the situation of China's 4.6 million Tibetans and their opposition to Chinese rule has been well documented in Western media, and the Dalai Lama is frequently labeled as a 'splittest' by the Xinhua News Agency, news stories about discontent in other Chinese border regions, particularly Xinjiang in northwest China, are relatively rare in the Western media," notes an authority on Chinese ethnic groups. "Their absence creates both a gap in Western knowledge of China and an opportunity to explore why some stories about China appear in the Western media while others don't."

Review Essay

A historian reviews works produced by American reporters in China since the 1930s: "Consistently, American journalists have favored the underdog—leading to favorable assessments of Chinese Communists during the 1940s, when they were rural guerrillas fighting the Japanese, and favorable assessments of Chinese democracy activists in the 1980s and 1990s who were contesting an entrenched Communist regime."

Note: The pinyin system for romanizing Chinese has been used in this volume, in some cases followed by the Wade-Giles equivalent for clarity. However, Seymour Topping's essay on covering the Chinese Civil War uses Wade-Giles to reflect accurately the place names used at that time.

Preface

Covering China

THE GREATEST CHALLENGE OF international reporting is interpretation: how do you explain one country and its culture to another? The task is always difficult, but the burdens and the consequences loom especially large when the two countries in question are China and the United States, whose long relationship in the 20th century has been marked by a lack of mutual comprehension that stretches from America's old missionary paternalism to the fears and fascinations of the present. That is why we have devoted this volume to the subject of "Covering China."

The subject has been especially appropriate since 1999, a year of three anniversaries that are bound to prompt reflection on both sides of the Pacific. The 80th anniversary of the May 4th movement, a surge of protest in 1919 that opposed Western domination, supported freedom of expression and helped give rise to the Chinese Communist Party, prompted reflection on the origins of the current regime in China. The 50th anniversary of the birth of the People's Republic of China encouraged consideration of where communism has brought China and the relationship between China and the United States. And the 10th anniversary of the democracy movement in Tiananmen Square and its suppression fostered questions about the state of freedom in China today.

"One aspect of a country's greatness," the historian Jonathan Spence has observed, "is surely its capacity to attract and retain the attention of others." For much of the 20th century, China has attracted the attention of American journalists, from the first China hands who covered an ancient country lurching into the 20th century to the chroniclers of the Chinese Civil War and World War II to the reporters who today explore the contradictions of China's economy. The essays collected here look at all of these different generations of American reporters. And, because it is impossible to understand the coverage of China without some grasp of the media scene inside China, we also look at elements of the Chinese media. Journalists' portraits of another country are usually influenced by the questions, concerns and conceptions they bring from their own land. That is certainly true of American reporting on China, and the same could be said of depictions of the United States in the Chinese media.

COVERING CHINA IS DIVIDED into three sections. "Histories" explores the events, anniversaries and processes that shape the media in China and American coverage of China. Jeffrey Wasserstrom listens to the echoes of the May 4th movement and shows how both orthodox Communists and activists can stake claims to its legacy. The China hands of the '30s and '40s are examined, in their many viewpoints, by Stephen MacKinnon. Seymour Topping contributes a memoir of covering the Chinese Civil War. Tsan-Kuo Chang looks at how American reporters covered China over the two decades when they were barred from the country. From Beijing in the 10th anniversary year of the democracy movement, Jaime FlorCruz looks at the state of the Chinese media and freedom of the press.

"Communicating" explores the challenges of explaining China to Americans and Americans to Chinese. Peter Conn reveals the too-little-known journalism of Pearl S. Buck, the novelist whose writings once defined China for so many Americans.
Carolyn Wakeman explores contemporary portrayals of China in the United States news media. Philip Cunningham, writing from Beijing, looks at Chinese media reactions to the Clinton scandal to understand Chinese depictions of the United States. Dai Qing examines Communist efforts to guide public opinion in the media, while Ying Chan evaluates the Hong Kong media's continuing status as a window between China and the West. In an interview, Orville Schell discusses the lessons learned in a life of writing about China and how he tries to impart them today as an educator.

"Issues" examines important stories now emerging in China that will matter to both journalists and China watchers. James Mann critiques the simplistic frames that too often shape American reporting on China. Jennifer Lin explores the changing worlds of Chinese women. From Hong Kong, Joyce Barnathan explains the difficulties of covering the Chinese economy. Wu Mei studies coverage of the Three Gorges dam to show how Chinese environmental stories fare in North American news media. Dru Gladney examines the little-covered story of ethnic unrest in northwest China.

In our review essay, Edward L. Farmer assays six major books on China by American journalists with an eye to understanding the consequences of American reporters' enduring preference for the cause of the underdog in Chinese society.

China presents to reporters a profound contradiction: media industries grow in ways that make the old Party press look anachronistic, yet democracy activists are thrown in prison. This is a bad combination. If journalism reaches its highest expression by carrying on the conversation of democracy, then the future of Chinese journalism is uncertain. Also cloudy is the future of reporting about China, which must explain prospects that can confound American beliefs about the relationship between media, markets and democracy.

The variety of points of view expressed in *Covering China* is a testament to the vigor of writing on China and a conviction that we hold about international reporting: When journalists are looking at a country as big and complex as China, it is important to see it from as many perspectives as possible. *Covering China* is our contribution to that effort.

—THE EDITORS

Part 1

HISTORIES

*Compared to the work done 60 years ago, today's China report-
ing is deeper and more professional. Nevertheless, the reporting
of 60 years ago was distinguished by a diversity of viewpoints
that is missing today.* —STEPHEN MACKINNON

1

Echoes of the May 4th Movement

Defenders of communist orthodoxy and democracy activists
both lay claim to a Chinese movement of 1919.

Jeffrey N. Wasserstrom

A WALKING TOUR OF BEIJING'S vast Tiananmen Square is a visually engaging introduction to the official history of the Revolution—a story long elevated to the status of holy narrative within the People's Republic of China. One key stop on such a tour is, of course, the Mao Mausoleum. Another is the Museum of Revolutionary History, which documents the efforts of Chairman Mao and the Chinese Communist Party that led to the "Liberation" of China in 1949. A third site that no historically minded visitor should miss is the Monument to the People's Heroes, a large obelisk whose base consists of a series of marble friezes depicting inspirational events from China's past.

Visitors interested in issues of freedom of speech should linger longest before the frieze devoted to the May 4th movement of 1919, which commemorates a struggle as famous in China as the Boston Tea Party is in the United States but which is still not well known in the West. It is possible to imagine, as I do in optimistic moments, that someday an additional statue will be placed in the Square, honoring what some activists have called the "New May 4th movement" of 1989. Until then, however, the marble frieze of the original May 4th movement will stand out as Tiananmen Square's most inspirational reminder of the usable past available to Chinese fighters for freedom.

3

What exactly does this frieze show? Your eye is drawn first to a young male orator, garbed in a university student's gown, lecturing down to an attentive group of onlookers: male and female students and men wearing the clothing of workers and peasants. We see a banner in the background, signifying that this is a rally. In the foreground, we see a female student holding a stack of leaflets and passing one to a worker.

The tableau highlights important facets of the May 4th movement, but perhaps inevitably, since the struggle was complex and open to competing interpretations, it obscures some aspects and effaces others. It is important to note what is emphasized and what is ignored, though, because the May 4th movement is an enduring symbol of great power, one invoked by defenders of the status quo (who note with pride the links between the protests of 1919 and the founding of the Chinese Communist Party in 1921) and by new generations of student protesters. The activists of 1989 are but the most recent to claim the legacy of 1919.

As the frieze suggests, one of the key components of May 4th was student activism. The struggle derives its name from the date in 1919 when educated youths marched through Beijing to express indignation over how China was being treated at the Paris Peace Conference after World War I, a war in which China sent 100,000 laborers to France to aid the Allied war effort. Despite providing such assistance to the victors in the Great War, the Treaty of Versailles proposed to transfer control of the Chinese province of Shandong from Germany to Japan. Furious students directed their anger at the foreign parties involved, particularly Japan, and also at China's "Three Traitorous Officials," whom they accused of greedily betraying their nation's interest to stay in Tokyo's good graces.

While it was predominately educated youths who took part in the original May 4th march—which ended in violence after students destroyed the house of a despised official and the police roughed up and arrested some protesters—the movement soon brought together different classes. It reached its peak in a "triple stoppage" in Shanghai that brought the great commercial center to a standstill for a week early in June. Students boycotted classes, workers struck and merchants refused to deal in Japanese goods. When news came later that all three official "traitors" had been dismissed from office, all arrested students had been released and the Chinese delegation had refused to sign the Treaty of Versailles, Chinese in many cities from many walks of life staged celebratory parades.

THE FRIEZE DEPICTS AN orator and a pamphleteer, one male and one female. This does justice to the historical record. May 4th was as much a campaign to arouse popular indignation and defend the right to speak out in public as it was an effort to change official policy. The protests of 1919 were among the earliest major political events in which students of both sexes played central roles.

The figure of the female activist in the frieze is also a reminder that in the May 4th movement students continually experimented with new media and put old ones to novel uses in their effort to inform and engage the masses. 1919 was one of the first years, though far from the last, when big character posters attacking corrupt officials seemed to cover every wall. It was one of the first years, though again not the last, when students organized lecture brigades to decry domestic abuses of power and foreign imperialism. It was a year when educated youths started new periodicals by the score, as they had done earlier that century in moments of crisis. And it was a year when some impassioned students followed in the footsteps of earlier generations of patriotic protesters by biting their fingers to write out slogans in blood.

Today, schoolchildren taken to Tiananmen to see the May 4th frieze know just where to place it on the official time line articulated in Communist textbooks, in which May 4th struggles stand proudly between the anti-dynastic agitations of 1911 and the progression toward Liberation in 1949. They know that Mao Zedong and Deng Xiaoping each took part in May 4th-era protest activities—Mao in China, Deng while studying in France, where his nickname, "Dr. Mimeograph," paid tribute to his enthusiastic work publicizing radical causes.

Some Chinese children are also aware, however, that the May 4th movement can be placed on an alternative time line and imbued with different meanings. They know there have always been some people, particularly intellectuals, who think of the May 4th movement as a fight for cultural renewal and democracy that still needs to be carried through to its logical conclusion. The legacy of 1919, in this vision, includes not just struggles that helped bring the Chinese Communist Party to power but also ones that have challenged its rule. It is this alternative May 4th that is harder to find hints of in the frieze.

ONE WAY TO BEGIN TO UNDERSTAND how official and unofficial images of May 4th diverge is to consider it in comparison with an episode familiar to Americans—the Boston Tea Party. Both events are famous; both involved a boycott. But there is another parallel worth noting. The May 4th movement, like the Boston Tea Party, has been infused with a complex mixture of both broadly democratic (and hence always potentially radical) as well as patriotic (and hence potentially more narrowly nationalistic) meanings. The Chinese struggle, like the American one, is treated in some contexts as having expressed intense love of country, in others as a manifestation of more universal yearnings for freedom; at times it is treated as a combination of both.

Yet the May 4th movement, unlike the Boston Tea Party, has also been viewed as an iconoclastic struggle for enlightenment and against the fetters of restrictive cultural traditions. The protests of 1919 involved some of the same people as the "New Culture" movement, which began in 1915 and was characterized by the founding of periodicals with names such as "New Youth." The New Culture movement was largely the work of intellectuals, but there was a concern in 1915, as there would be in 1919, with reaching out to the masses. This manifested itself in the interest the new journals showed in promoting the development of a "plain speech" writing style to replace the inaccessible formalistic prose then typically favored by the literary elite.

New Culture leaders published forceful attacks on outmoded stylistic conventions. Their polemics combined pragmatic suggestions (authors should avoid allusions to arcane canonical works, they said, and should feel freer to make use of popular sayings and proverbs) with rhetorical calls for the formation of a symbolic Army of Literary Revolution (to march behind a banner emblazoned with slogans such as "Destroy the outmoded, showy, classical literature and construct a fresh and sincere literature of realism"). Some New Culture writers, such as Lu Xun, put these ideals into practice in stories adapted from popular folktales, essays filled with vernacular sayings, and satirical writings about pretentious scholars who quoted Confucius and Mencius on the need to be benevolent toward all human beings but failed to care about the suffering of ordinary people.

Above all, New Culture activists attacked certain traditions, including an array of customs they associated with "Confucianism" that placed men above women and made young people of both sexes subservient to their elders. New Culture activists called for an end to all this and urged China's youth to learn from the best things foreign cultures had to offer while embracing individualistic forms of self-expression.

The New Culture aspects of May 4th are often marginalized within official narratives and are hard to find in the frieze as well. Male and female figures appear there, but without any indication that the May 4th activists, including Mao, developed a powerful critique of patriarchy. In addition, the May 4th-era activists' emphasis on individualism is missing from the frieze. The faces on the frieze have a sameness, a common fixity of expression, that suggest a homogeneity that fits in with a patriotic reading of 1919—but obscures the fact that May 4th was a complex set of interrelated struggles for different sorts of liberation.

IN LIGHT OF ALL THIS, there is good reason for anyone concerned with China's ongoing struggle for freedom to take note of the May 4th movement and its divergent meanings, especially in 1999, which will inevitably be a year of politically charged anniversaries. Commemorations often illuminate contemporary situations. Soon, efforts will be made to mark the passage of 80 years since the first May 4th protest, of 50 since "Liberation," of 10 since the Beijing and Chengdu massacres of 1989. How each of these moments is or is not commemorated in the People's Republic of China will tell us a great deal about the current state of that nation.

We may learn much about how Jiang Zemin sees his regime's place in history by watching how ceremonies commemorating the country's founding deal with Mao and Deng. Similarly, we may learn much about the present by observing the state's response to unofficial attempts by family members to honor the memory of the worker and student martyrs of 1989. But it is the treatment of May 4th that may be the most revealing of all.

Ultimately, the events of 1919 are symbolically tied to those of 1949 and 1989. Observances of the May 4th anniversary will inevitably shed light on contemporary understandings of several historical turning points in China. After all, since 1949, each of China's leaders has based his claim to legitimacy in part on the link between the May 4th movement and the Chinese Communist Party. But at key moments in the struggle of 1989, student activists challenged the notion that the Party represents the legacy of 1919. When Wang Dan and other protesters gathered in Tiananmen Square in 1989 to commemorate the 70th anniversary of the protests of 1919, they upstaged official observances being held simultaneously nearby. And when the activists charged that radical change was needed to get the Revolution back on track, they stood near the May 4th frieze.

The students of 1989 thus used May 4th imagery to question the very legitimacy of the Chinese Communist Party. Ironically, many of the old men who would defend the killings of 1989 were Party veterans who cut their political teeth doing just the sorts of things portrayed on the marble frieze. More ironically, many first developed a taste for political action by speaking out for freedom and against corruption in much the same manner as the protesters of 1989. These ironies added a special sting to the protests of that year, and they continue to have a political bite. After all, though Jiang Zemin was not a member of the original May 4th generation, he was active in student movements of the 1940s that were sometimes called "New May 4th" struggles by their supporters.

One key question raised in 1989 was simple: does the Chinese Communist Party have a right to present itself as a defender of the ideals of 1919 or has it forfeited forever this claim? The massacres and mass arrests put an end to public debate of this and so many other questions, but the symbolic power of May 4th and its ability to stand for different things to different people has not diminished.

Eighty years after the events of 1919, in a year of anniversaries when many of the debates closed off a decade ago are likely to be reopened with renewed vigor, the May 4th legacy should matter to everyone in the outside world who is interested in China's prospects for becoming a freer place. Within China, to those struggling to create a more open society or simply dreaming of becoming part of one, the legacy of 1919 also matters. There, it can never be frozen in marble or relegated to an officially commemorated event of the distant past. The legacy of 1919 is a living thing, something to struggle for in moments like this one, when corrupt power holders and official gags keep China from becoming the kind of place envisioned by the heroes and heroines whose faces are etched on the Tiananmen monument.

Jeffrey N. Wasserstrom teaches history at Indiana University. He is the associate editor of the American Historical Review *and author of* Student Protests in Twentieth-Century China.

2

The "Romantic" Generation

*The old China hands left a legacy that helps
and hurts American journalism.*

Stephen MacKinnon

OVERLY ROMANTIC REPORTING about China in the 1930s and 1940s, a vital period in Chinese political history and Sino-American relations, launched the roller coaster ride that has characterized the U.S.-China relationship and news media coverage ever since. For the first time, the U.S. press gave extensive coverage to a non-Western, nonwhite society in the throes of revolutionary change.

While the era opened with expressions of growing empathy for the ordinary, impoverished Chinese of Pearl Buck's *The Good Earth*, by the late 1930s, with China at war with Japan, reporting became more political and romantic in support of Chinese nationalism. The "special relationship" with China turned sour unexpectedly in the late 1940s as the Communists came to power and relations deteriorated to the point of war over Korea in 1950. The adjustment was cathartic, giving full play to the emotional dimension of the relationship that has produced to this day wild swings between positive and negative imagery and public opinion about China.

Certain patterns in China reporting have repeated themselves since these crucial years. One is cheerleading: In the 1980s, and especially during the spring of 1989, the U.S. media hailed Chinese democracy

9

and capitalism in a manner reminiscent of U.S. support for Chiang Kai-shek's United Front in the late 1930s. In both cases, excessive zeal in reporting created an atmosphere ripe for eventual disappointments. Another is American politicians' conscious cultivation of the legacy of the journalists of the 1930s. When President Nixon went to China in 1972, he made a point of bringing with him as many of the old China hands as possible, including Tillman Durdin and Theodore White. When President Clinton visited China in 1998, he read Edgar Snow's *Red Star Over China* in preparation and visited the Snow memorial at Beijing University.

EMULATION OF THE "ROMANTIC" generation of reporters who pioneered in bringing China to the front pages of the U.S. press is ironic because, in retrospect, the great strength of China reporting of the 1930s and 1940s was diversity of viewpoint. Most of the daily and feature writing was produced by men and women who arrived in China "by accident," as they themselves liked to say. Unlike their more professionally experienced and linguistically prepared contemporaries who covered momentous events in Europe, the China crowd were refugees from the Great Depression, attracted by the promise of adventure in a mysterious country and rumors of job opportunities. Jobs were especially important to women because the chances of breaking into journalism in China were much better than in Europe.

The majority of the adventure seekers were middle-class sons and daughters from California and the Midwest, like Annalee Jacoby, Emily Hahn, Helen Foster Snow (who wrote under the name Nym Wales) and Betty Graham. Arriving early were key figures like Edgar Snow, F. McCracken "Mac" Fisher (United Press) and Tillman Durdin (*The New York Times*), whose initial planned stay of a few months turned into 15 years. These three cut their teeth as stringers in 1929-30, then found real jobs on local English-language publications and eventually worked their way up to bureau chiefs for major organizations. The University of Missouri's School of Journalism had an unusually large contingent of graduates in China and Japan—known affectionately as the Missouri "mafia." There were a few, like Peggy Durdin, who were from missionary families and spoke the Chinese language. But Theodore White in 1940 was probably the first to prepare formally by studying Chinese and the country at Harvard before taking off for Shanghai.

China attracted the young and adventurous because the cost of living was low, the atmosphere was exotic, and jobs for the educated foreigner more plentiful than back home. New arrivals landed in sprawling and exciting treaty port cities like Shanghai or Tianjin, which were more cosmopolitan than most midwestern cities and Westernized to the point that English was used widely. Travel in China was unrestricted but not for the faint of heart, given the lack of infrastructure and primitive nature of the economy. But if banditry and social unrest made the countryside dangerous for the Chinese, foreigners enjoyed protected, privileged status because of China's subservient economic and political status internationally. Moreover, the Chinese people seemed open and accessible.

Urban China in the 1930s was in a period of unprecedented receptivity and interest in Western culture and society. Chinese students were returning from the United States and Europe to staff bureaucracies and pursue professional careers, including journalism. A mutual dependence grew up between young American journalists and Chinese intellectuals. Young Chinese staffed offices and acted as translators, becoming Americans' principal news sources and guides to the Chinese scene. Chinese colleagues of American journalists gained experience used later in Chinese journalism, good salaries and cover of foreign protection for a variety of political activities. Typical was Liu Zunqi, who worked first for Harold Isaacs in Shanghai and then during World War II for the U.S. government as head of the Chinese staff of McCracken Fisher's Office of War Information in Chongqing. After the establishment of the People's Republic of China, Liu was one of the founders of Guangming ribao and China Daily in Beijing.

MANY OF THE YOUNG American journalists were drawn by their Chinese counterparts into the political movements of the time. For example, through Huang Hua (future foreign minister of the People's Republic of China), Edgar Snow, Helen Foster Snow and McCracken Fisher became active participants in the December 9, 1935, student demonstrations that urged Chiang Kai-shek to fight the Japanese and set the stage for a much broader wave of mass demonstrations across the country.

Young American adventurers were thrust into a momentous period in modern Chinese history. The atmosphere was exciting, romantic and ideal for the launching of a career as a foreign correspondent: there was growing American public interest in China, paralleled by increasing business, missionary and philanthropic involvement.

Contributing diversity to the growing coverage of China in the 1930s were the political passion and ideological commitment of some of the more experienced new arrivals. Agnes Smedley, Anna Louise Strong, Freda Utley and Frank Glass, for example, arrived with political positions already shaped by an activist history of involvement in struggles in the United States and elsewhere. Missouri-born Smedley—whose activism in support of Indian independence from Britain and Margaret Sanger's fight for birth control had landed her in prison in New York in 1918—spent a period of political exile in Germany, where she wrote for the left-leaning *Frankfurter Zeitung*. She went to Shanghai in 1929. Initially, Smedley saw Shanghai as a way station for continuing her fight to end British colonialism in India. But then she contacted the underground Chinese communist movement, wrote a book about the Long March, and her career as the John Reed of the Chinese revolution was launched. There were also advocate journalists on the right (as well as editors at home like Henry Luce). Maurice Votaw, an ex-missionary and a virulent anti-communist, was a strong supporter of Chiang Kai-shek. He eventually worked for the Nationalist government's own news agency during World War II.

Others like Edgar Snow, Helen Foster Snow or Jack Belden, who arrived in China in a relatively apolitical state, developed a missionary-like concern for the plight of the ordinary downtrodden Chinese after witnessing their hardships and struggles. Covering a social and political revolution coterminous with an epic war against the Japanese eventually produced deep emotional responses and turned some into advocacy journalists. Snow went on to break the news blackout on the Chinese Communists by visiting them in their cave headquarters in 1936 and writing *Red Star Over China*.

Bracketed by advocacy journalism on the right and left were figures like A.T. Steele, Durdin, J.B. Powell, Randall Gould and others who prided themselves on their "objectivity." Durdin and Steele had witnessed and written about the Nanking Massacre of 1937, Durdin for the *Times* and Steele for the *Herald Tribune* and *Chicago Daily News*. They often met socially and swapped intelligence with U.S. consular and embassy officials.

AFTER WAR BETWEEN China and Japan was formally declared in 1937, the gap between the more politically committed and "objective" journalists like Steele and Durdin closed. The overall sense of community among American reporters was strong, nowhere more than in Hankou in 1938, when the sprawling central Yangzi commercial center was under Japanese siege for 10 months as the defacto capital of wartime China. Once a week, above Rosie's Restaurant, a meeting was held of the "last ditchers club," made up of journalists of all persuasions, who were joined by military attachés like Evans Carlson, Frank Dorn and Joseph Stilwell, diplomat John Davies, photographer Robert Capa, filmmaker Joris Ivens and celebrity writers W.H. Auden and Christopher Isherwood. The experience of bearing witness to the heroic United Front struggle of the Chinese against the Japanese generated an intense camaraderie that crossed professional and political lines.

Shared also were the constraints of censorship and control exercised by gatekeeping editors in the United States. Comparatively speaking, the China reporters of the 1930s and 1940s were relatively autonomous in choice and framing of stories. Editorial directions were infrequent, mostly because communication was technologically difficult. Then, as now, human-interest stories received priority, especially if a hometown connection could be developed—no matter how trivial or farfetched. It was considered a good idea to tie a story about hundreds of Chinese killed in a famine riot to the fact that a missionary from Indiana had his window broken. American reporters could use their privileged position as foreigners to evade Chinese government censorship, but Chinese press controls were still annoying. The chief censor, Hollington Tong, a University of Missouri graduate who had once worked for *The New York Times*, used his knowledge of the ways of American journalism to plug leaks in the system and rather effectively control access to people in high places. Holly, as he was known to the Americans, was not universally loved nor invited to the dinner parties above Rosie's.

JAMES RESTON AND OTHERS HAVE observed that American foreign correspondents are trained to report events and they do this efficiently and well. They are weak, however, in reporting important intellectual and ideological trends in the country to which they are posted. Much of the blame for this tendency lies with gatekeeping editors back home who demand "hard news." In the China reporting of the 1930s and 1940s, when the events of the Sino-Japanese war dominated coverage, the China journalists rarely explored the crypto-fascist quality of Nationalist ideology or political currents within the Chinese communist movement. The Communist purges of the 1942-44 period, for example, which Mao Zedong used to consolidate his power base, were completely missed.

Contributing to both diversity of viewpoint and romantic tendencies was the relative isolation of the 1930s China reporter. Most of them lived in China for years at a time with few home leaves, putting them out of touch with the public mood and the mindset of editors back home. Even within China communication was erratic and slow. In contrast to the information overload the journalist faces today, the China reporter of the 1930s wrote more single-source stories that were difficult to corroborate factually. Isolation and primitive communications produced great variety in content because reporters were more limited in choice of "facts" and hence able to indulge their biases about China. Tremendous disparities in factual reporting about China appeared in the U.S. press, as in the case of contemporary coverage of the Communists' Long March in 1934-35.

The relative autonomy of the China reporters in the 1930s gave them greater freedom to be empathetic and romantic in reporting about China—and to choose *their* China. The Chinas they chose to write about varied politically a great deal, from right to left to the frivolous. For some, China meant struggling peasants and sweatshop workers; for others, the Nationalist ruling elites; and for still others, the seemingly exotic and mysterious customs of the people.

THE DIFFERENCES between the romantic generation of China reporters from the 1930s and 1940s and the midcareer professionals who report today from Beijing, Shanghai and Hong Kong are obvious. Perhaps because they are given less autonomy by editors, reporters who serve the mass media market today have less choice of subject matter. (Although a distinction needs to be made between general-interest reporting and the recent proliferation of specialized media outlets for stories on sports, business and professional interests such as law, medicine and science.) Given the post-Cold War environment, it is not surprising that ideological commitment is no longer an issue. Advocacy reporting is limited to the issues of human rights, the environment and Tibet. Being kept on a tight leash by editors back home inevitably produces more of a herd mentality, especially around big events like a presidential visit or the return of Hong Kong.

Because of the tight controls that are applied to journalists by the public security and foreign ministries, travel in China is more restricted than it was 60 years ago. Frustration is heightened by the fact that, physically and linguistically, travel is otherwise much easier and safer. Deportation, searches and harassing surveillance are much more of a real threat than they were in the 1930s. Thus a return to the old-fashioned leaky censorship of Hollington Tong would be a welcome improvement.

The China reporter today is much better prepared and more professionally experienced, having some command over the Chinese language and some record of formal study of Chinese history, culture and politics. A few are daughters and sons of China scholars; some, such as Fox Butterfield and Orville Schell, have graduate degrees in Chinese studies. Most have worked in the U.S. media before arriving in China. There are many more Chinese-American reporters. The cumulative effect of all this is a much higher level of professionalism. Gone is the crypto-racist, paternalist approach of the worst reporting from the 1930s and 1940s.

Today, among American journalists in China, the sense of community is different from what it was half a century ago, and the competitive instinct is stronger. Common problems with Chinese censorship and gatekeeping editors back home bring journalists together. Liaisons are more professionally than socially based, in contrast to the more clubby intimacy of the past. And, of course, since the Vietnam War, information swapping with government officials is greatly reduced.

JUST AS IMPORTANT, however, are the continuities with the 1930s and 1940s that persist. China is still an exotic and inscrutable place in the American public's mind. Editors at home still look for the strange human-interest story with an American connection. Less obvious perhaps is the fact that the China journalist today, as in the 1940s, continues to be a prisoner of the emotional roller coaster swings in the U.S.-China relationship from positive to negative and back again. In 1998, the drastic change in image of China's current leader, Jiang Zemin, from negative to positive is a case in point.

The symbiotic relationship between the Chinese and foreign press continues. China reporting still reflects the prejudices and concerns of the urban Chinese intellectuals who make up a disproportionate number of sources. The travails and growing sophistication of the Chinese press during the 1980s contributed to an improvement in U.S. coverage of China. At the beginning of the decade, U.S. reporting, which was remarkably homogeneous and derivative of Chinese views, blamed the Cultural Revolution for all of China's contemporary ills. By the late 1980s and throughout the 1990s, sustained access to reliable sources and experience gave coverage greater variety and depth. Nevertheless, not for want of trying but because of censorship and heavy-handed control of access, coverage of the rural economic and social issues has been very difficult, as it was in the 1930s and 1940s. Inevitably, the focus of contemporary U.S. reporting on China remains urban. Increased attention is thus given to questions of coastal economic growth and political dissent. Urban bias, however, has led to such mistakes as an overestimation of the success of population-control efforts in the country as a whole.

Such weaknesses must be weighed against the reporting of previous generations. Compared to the work done 60 years ago, today's China reporting is deeper and more professional. Nevertheless, the reporting of 60 years ago was distinguished by a diversity of viewpoints that is missing today. Decades after the heyday of the old China hands, American reporting on China both benefits and suffers from their romantic legacy.

Stephen MacKinnon, a professor of history at Arizona State University, is co-author of a biography of Agnes Smedley and China Reporting—An Oral History of American Journalism in the 1930s and 1940s.

3

Covering the Chinese Civil War

Lessons that echoed from Nanking to Saigon

Seymour Topping

IN THE EARLY MORNING HOURS OF April 24, 1949, the capital of Chiang Kai-shek's Nationalist China lay prostrate before Communist troops storming across the Yangzi River. Nanking had been abandoned by its Nationalist army garrison. The municipal police had fled. The massive gates of the walled city of 1.2 million people were ajar and unguarded, mobs roamed the streets looting shops and homes of Nationalist officials, barricades were up at the foreign embassies, and flames from torched government buildings reddened the low-hanging clouds.

At 3 o'clock that morning, after roaming the frightened city to report on the chaotic scenes, Bill Kuan, a Chinese reporter for Agence France Presse, and I were in my jeep, driving down the Chungshan Lu thoroughfare toward the city's Northwest Gate. We had learned that a citizens' Peace Preservation Committee was going to the gate to meet the approaching Communists. As I drove slowly along the empty and darkened boulevard, there was a shout of "Halt" in Chinese. From the sides of the road, two soldiers with rifles aimed converged on us. "Who are you?" one asked as he held a flashlight on us. Kuan replied, "I am a correspondent of the French news agency, and he is from the American Associated Press." "American!" the soldier exclaimed, looking at me intently. "Do you know who we are? We are soldiers of the

People's Liberation Army." The two were the point of the first Communist column into Nanking.

We were taken down the road to a Communist officer who was urging his exhausted column of troops to move quickly into the city. To stop a further torching of the city, the column had come through the Northwest Gate at a forced march. The harassed officer impatiently ordered us to turn our Jeep around, and gratefully we sped back into the city, past the burning Judicial Yuan (the supreme court) to the telegraph office. There, Kuan and I flipped a coin to decide who would file first. Kuan won and sent a three-word flash: "Reds take Nanking." My packed 60-word dispatch followed. Immediately after, the cable between Nanking and Shanghai was severed. When Kuan's flash reached the AFP desk in Paris, the editors waited for additional details, which did not come until morning when radio transmission opened. My own dispatch had gone out on the AP wire, luck bestowing a beat. At dawn, when Kuan and I emerged from the telegraph office after filing complete stories, the Communists were in occupation of the city that Chiang Kai-shek had made his capital in 1928.

The fall of Nanking was the climax of a civil war mainly fought on remote battlefields rarely reached by journalists. From 1927 to 1937, Chiang had waged a war of extermination against elusive Communist guerrillas led by Mao Tse-tung. Little was known abroad about the Communists until the mid-1930s when Edgar Snow, a young American reporter for the *New York Sun* and the *London Daily Herald*, clandestinely reached Yenan, Mao's refuge in remote northwest China, and subsequently wrote his epic *Red Star Over China*. Mao and Chiang joined in an uneasy coalition in 1937 to resist Japanese invaders, but the civil war erupted again soon after the end of World War II. Now hundreds of thousands of Communist troops were crossing the broad Yangzi against feeble resistance on a front extending from central China to Nanking and turning east toward Shanghai, which fell on May 27. Chiang was in Taiwan promising that one day he would retake the mainland. Mao was in Peiping, the ancient northern capital formerly known as Peking, and in control of most of the mainland.

WHEN I ARRIVED IN PEIPING IN October 1946 as a stringer for the International News Service, with the title of chief correspondent for north China and Manchuria (retainer: $50 a month), the flash point of the renewed civil war was in Manchuria. I was still in the uniform of an infantry captain, having taken terminal leave in the Philippines after three years of army service. In Manila I had scrounged a string with INS. I was 24 years old, and my only newspaper experience had been on the *Columbia Missourian,* the student newspaper at the School of Journalism of the University of Missouri. In Peiping I rented a room in the College of Chinese Studies, started taking language lessons, got a Chinese tailor to make me a pin-striped suit and shortly afterwards filed my first war dispatch.

Peiping was a beguiling walled city. On its narrow cobbled streets, overburdened camels and peasant carts mingled with American-made trucks of the Nationalist garrison and polished limousines of the foreign consulates. A small group of correspondents was based in Peiping, most of them living luxuriously with Chinese servants in charming compounds. They benefited from the presence of Executive Headquarters, which was established in 1945 by Gen. George Marshall, special envoy of President Truman, to assist in bringing about a cease-fire in the civil war. Like the other correspondents, I soon was traveling on the planes of truce teams sent out by the American, Nationalist and Communist branches of the headquarters through Inner Mongolia, north China and Manchuria.

I approached the other correspondents, veterans all, with ill-concealed awe. The Americans included the celebrated Arch Steele of the *Herald Tribune,* Benjamin Welles, son of Under Secretary of State Sumner Welles, and James Burke of Time-Life, who later toppled to his death over a Himalayan precipice when he slipped while taking photographs. My agency competitors were John Roderick, a jovial and highly skilled professional, and Reynolds Packard of the United Press, the agency's chief correspondent in the Mediterranean during World War II. They provided a hard school for a novice correspondent.

Packard, a fleshy, rollicking man, felt he had to write to please the "Kansas City Milkman," the title of a book he later wrote exposing the foibles of his news agency. The moment of truth came for Pack when he was fired not long after he filed a story picked up from the imaginative Chinese press about a human-headed spider. I hinted to my colleagues that the parsimonious INS, always downholding cable tolls, had instructed me not to match Pack's story—which had caused a sensation around the world—unless I could find a spider with two human heads. In general, the foreign correspondents, unable to move freely in the immensity of the Chinese hinterland, were overly dependent on the unreliable Chinese press and the propaganda broadcasts of the Communist Yenan Radio.

Roderick was a canny competitor. Once in 1947, the correspondents flew to Changchun, the old Japanese capital of the puppet state of Manchukuo. The city, encircled by the Communists, was under fire and would soon fall. After visiting the front, we drew lots to determine the order in which our dispatches would be sent by the primitive cable office. We slept that night on the floor of one of the cavernous buildings of the puppet government that had been looted by Chinese peasants and at daybreak trooped to the cable office to check on our dispatches. Cunningly, Roderick had marked his copy "urgent" without telling us, but to no avail. Walter Bosshard, of the *Neue Zurcher Zeitung*, dean of the Peiping correspondents, had casually allowed his dispatch to be filed last explaining that he was not up against a deadline. The telegraph clerk had taken the last dispatch deposited, sitting on top of the pile, and Bosshard's cable had gone first. The Swiss fox had scored another beat.

ON AN EARLIER VISIT TO Changchun, I had taken the train south to Mukden, the principal city of Manchuria, in the company of Jules Joelson of Agence France Presse and Vladimir Drozdov, a Russian reporter. When Communist guerrillas blew up the railroad tracks, we huddled in the stalled unheated train for a day without food. I then noticed that Joelson was jealously husbanding a paper bag. It contained a large jar of caviar that he had picked up in the White Russian exile community at Harbin near the Soviet border. Soon the three of us were digging out handfuls of caviar, ruining my taste for the precious stuff for years to come. Later that day we rolled on to Mukden, where I spent Christmas at the beginning of a Communist siege during which thousands of civilians, subsisting on tree bark and cattle fodder, died of starvation. Nationalist troops and officials, as well as the few foreigners living in hotels and various missions, obtained food from relief transport planes that managed to reach the city.

Roderick had distinguished himself in 1945 by spending seven months in Yenan reporting on the Communist leadership at a critical political juncture. Premier Chou En-lai was at the time in Chungking, the Nationalist wartime capital, negotiating with Nationalist leaders under American auspices for a peace agreement, which neither side, in fact, wanted. An opening for correspondents to visit blockaded Yenan was made in July 1944 when a U.S. military observer group, known as the Dixie Mission, was sent to Communist headquarters. The presence of the mission facilitated visits by a succession of correspondents, initially by those, such as Teddy White of *Time* magazine, based in Chungking, and then a considerable number of others. This arrangement provided Mao with his first access to the world press since the Snow visit.

Two months after my arrival in Peiping I flew to Yenan, where in interviews with Communist leaders I gained insights into the nature of Mao's revolution. In 1934, under attack by Chiang Kai-shek's armies, Mao had led the remnants of his guerrilla forces on a 6,000 mile "Long March" to a narrow valley of Shensi, where they created a base of some 10,000 caves dug out of the sides of the loess hills. Although still blockaded by Nationalist troops, the Communists had succeeded in broadly extending their "Liberated Areas" largely by rallying the support of the peasantry. This land policy was a key to the eventual Communist triumph. Over time, landlords and village officials of the Kuomintang Party, the political arm of the Nationalists, many of them notoriously corrupt, were ruthlessly purged, often executed, and their holdings distributed to the land-hungry peasants. Years later, I was not surprised when the peasants who had struggled so hard to obtain their individual plots were compelled to surrender them to communes. The Party leaders I met in the caves of Yenan never concealed their intent to transform China by stages into a Communist state. They differed with Stalin who tried unsuccessfully to persuade them to adopt the orthodox Leninist strategy of basing their revolution on the urban proletariat rather than the peasantry.

MOST OF THE CORRESPONDENTS in China operated out of Nanking and Shanghai. After six months in Peiping, INS rewarded me with a staff job and I moved into the Nanking press hostel. The company was distinguished. *The New York Times* was represented by Tillman Durdin, who reported on the Japanese Rape of Nanking in 1937, and Henry Lieberman, who, from 1946 to 1949 while on the China mainland and then for the next five years from Hong Kong, filed altogether the most complete press account of the civil war. Christopher Rand, of the *Herald Tribune*, another resident of the press hostel, was conspicuous not only for his fine reporting but also as the press corps' most colorful character. A self-styled Buddhist, wearing a rope for a belt and tennis shoes, he sometimes wrote his copy standing up with his portable on the mantelpiece. His copy was rather wooden until he found a voice in dictation, which produced stylish copy that took him from the *Tribune* to success at *The New Yorker*.

The largest number of reporters were based in Shanghai. Most lived, some with families and a few with White Russian or Chinese mistresses, in the foreign correspondents club, which occupied the top four stories of the Broadway Mansions, a high rise overlooking the foul Soochow Creek. Those mingling at the penthouse bar included Bob Shaplen of *Newsweek*, Waldo Drake of the *Los Angeles Times*, Pepper Martin of the *New York Post*, Phil Potter of *The Baltimore Sun*, John Hersey of *Time*, Spencer Moosa of the Associated Press, Keyes Beech of the *Chicago Daily News*, Clyde Farnsworth of Scripps Howard, Walter Sullivan of *The New York Times*, Roy Rowan, the *Life* photographer, and many others whose bylines were well known. After the Communists occupied Shanghai, from the balcony of the bar in what by then was a virtually empty club, I watched Nationalist bombers carrying out random bombing of the city.

From Peiping, Nanking and Shanghai, the correspondents traveled throughout the Nationalist-held areas of China chronicling catastrophic economic conditions and the crumbling of Nationalist control under Communist pressure. While American correspondents were critical of the failings of the Nationalists, only a very few, notably Edgar Snow, Anna Louise Strong and Israel Epstein, leaned ideologically in their reporting to the Communists. Strong was granted a number of interviews by Mao, including one, widely quoted, in which he denounced the United States as a "paper tiger" and predicted that the atom bomb would not be used again. By January 1947, the Communist areas were closed to Western correspondents. With the failure of his mediation mission, Gen. Marshall had packed up Executive Headquarters in Peiping. The Communists, resentful of U.S. military aid to the Nationalist cause, saw no gain in giving access to American correspondents.

However, in February 1947, Jack Belden, a brilliant war correspondent who worked at times for the United Press and Time, did manage to slip into the "Liberated Areas." He made a foray across the North China Plain, some 300 miles from Peiping, to the headquarters of Liu Po-cheng, the famous one-eyed Communist general. Traveling by truck and peasant carts, Belden spent weeks in the Communist areas collecting material for his book, *China Shakes the World*. The book, published in 1949 and comparable to Snow's *Red Star Over China*, sold poorly: Reporting from China that gave credit to Communist reforms in the villages had, with the onset of the Cold War, become suspect in the United States.

The correspondents in Peiping progressively became more isolated in 1948 as Communist forces descended from Manchuria into north China. Driven back in 1946 by Nationalist divisions airlifted by the U.S. Air Force into Manchuria, the Communists had regrouped and taken the offensive. They were armed with Japanese weapons taken from depots left to them by the Russians who had disarmed the Japanese army of occupation. Chiang Kai-shek made his chronic blunder of positioning his divisions in the towns and cities. Maneuvering in the countryside, the legendary Communist commander Lin Piao successively isolated the Nationalist positions, wiped out more than 30 divisions and captured mountains of American equipment. Nationalist surrender in north China followed, and Communist troops occupied Peiping on January 31, 1949. Four weeks later, the *People's Daily*, the official Communist organ, published a decree forbidding the resident 17 foreign correspondents from gathering or sending news. Among those blacklisted was A. Doak Barnett of the *Chicago Daily News*, who later became one of the most prominent historians of the era. On October 1, when Mao proclaimed the People's Republic in Peiping, there were no functioning American journalists in the city.

IN DECEMBER 1948, BEFORE MAO moved to Peiping, I undertook what may have been the last attempt to reach his remote headquarters. I had left INS for the AP and was working under Nanking bureau chief Harold Milks. Boarding a railway box car I traveled to Pengpu, about 100 miles north of Nanking. There I entered an Italian Jesuit Mission to await the anticipated Communist entry into the town, which had been largely evacuated by the Nationalists. When New Year's Day passed and the Communists did not come, I crossed no-man's-land. At a road block, I was taken by Communist guerrillas. By horseback I was led for the next three days to a headquarters in Hwai-Hai region, where Communist and Nationalist forces were locked in an enormous battle. Near the headquarters, I was held in a peasant's grain storage shed and questioned by a political commissar before my request for an interview with Mao went forward. On January 7, the answer came: "Return. You are in a war zone. It is not convenient for you to proceed." I was then escorted back to no-man's-land and crossed into the Nationalist lines. The message was clear. The honeymoon with American correspondents was over.

A few days after I left the Communist headquarters on the Hwaipei Plain, the battle there—the most decisive of the civil war—ended. The Communists had engaged a Nationalist force of about the same size as theirs but much better equipped with tanks and artillery and in command of the air. Yet in 65 days the Communists, employing once again their strategy of maneuver against fixed Nationalist positions, wiped out 56 Nationalist divisions, including the Armored Corps, a force comprising 556,000 men. In the disasters on the Hwaipei Plain and in Manchuria, the Nationalists lost all of their 39 American-equipped and trained divisions.

These stunning Communist victories have been attributed to skilled leadership, the high morale of their well-indoctrinated troops and support of the peasantry. But account should also be taken of the major factor cited by Maj. Gen. David Barr, chief of the U.S. military advisory group. Barr reported to Washington, "The military debacles, in my opinion, can all be attributed to the world's worst leadership." Corruption and dishonesty throughout the Nationalist army, Barr said, led to complete loss of the will to fight.

During the first two days of the Communist occupation of Nanking, I was confined for two days to the Associated Press compound after a Communist patrol entered the house and questioned a servant about my activities. Chester Ronning, the chargé d'affaires of the Canadian Embassy, the father of my fiancée, Audrey, who had been evacuated earlier with members of her family, slipped food packages to me through the barbed-wire fence. Thereafter, however, I was free, like the few other correspondents in Nanking, to move freely about the city and file dispatches.

But news coverage of the civil war dried up with the occupation of Peiping, Nanking and Shanghai. Some correspondents hung on in Nanking and Shanghai for a time but were denied access to Communist officials and forbidden to travel. Coverage of the last battles on the mainland in central and south China shifted to Hong Kong. Six months after the fall of Nanking, I left for Hong Kong on the first evacuation ship out of Shanghai, the General W. H. Gordon.

With my departure, my Chinese assistant, J. C. Jao, a graduate of the School of Journalism at the University of Missouri, took over coverage of Nanking. Harold Milks had left before the fall of Nanking on home leave, believing that a Communist attack on the capital was not imminent. Some months later, Jao was brought into a Communist indoctrination course and interrogated by the police. He informed Fred Hampson, the AP bureau chief in Shanghai, that he was resisting taking a job with the Communists writing anti-American propaganda.

On February 21, 1951, Peking promulgated a decree for punishment of "counterrevolutionaries." It resulted in the following two years in the execution of at least 1 million people. Jao, named a counterrevolutionary and accused of espionage, disappeared in the purge.

From Hong Kong I flew in late January 1950 to Hainan Island, a lush green territory only 500 square miles smaller than Taiwan off the south China coast, that was still held by the Nationalists. From the roof of the French Catholic Mission, I watched Nationalist bombers attacking Lin Piao's troops on the coastal side of the Hainan Strait 10 miles away, where they were preparing to assault the island. On April 17, Lin Piao's troops swarmed ashore on 160 junks, and Communist guerrillas struck from the interior. It was the last major operation of the civil war. Taiwan remained as the distant objective of the Communists.

THERE WAS A VITAL LESSON TO be learned by the United States from its involvement in the civil war, a lesson that could have spared the nation incalculable grief. We should have learned that firepower in a civil war is not enough to prop up a regime that lacks popular support. That lesson was not absorbed because in some measure the reporting of the China correspondents was obscured by the confused political debate and uproar at home on how to respond to Soviet expansionism. The China lobby, with its cries of "Who lost China?" and its scapegoat denunciations of Gen. Joseph Stilwell, Gen. Marshall and State Department officials, diverted blame from the Chiang Kai-shek government where it belonged.

In 1950 when I opened the AP bureau in Saigon, American officials told me that the China experience had no relevance to the Vietnam War because the French had more effective firepower. In two years in Vietnam I learned that was not true. In 1963, when I returned to Vietnam for *The New York Times*, in discussing the French experience with Americans generals, I was told it was not relevant because the United States had more firepower. Perhaps, the lesson was learned eventually in Vietnam decades after the Chinese Civil War.

Seymour Topping is administrator of the Pulitzer Prizes and professor of international journalism at Columbia University. He is the former managing editor of The New York Times *and author of* Journey Between Two Chinas *and* The Peking Letter, A Novel of the Chinese Civil War, *which will be published this fall by PublicAffairs.*

4

China from Here and There

*More than two decades of closed borders
and narrowed vision*

Tsan-Kuo Chang

REPORTING CHINA HAS NEVER been an easy aspect of Sino-American relations, especially when the United States and China tend to look at each other from very different points of view. The range of vision in the political landscapes between here and there has led journalists, both Chinese and American, to survey selective elements of the same reality and interpret them according to disparate presumptions. From Washington to Beijing, the result is often conflict and confrontation in journalistic spirit and practices.

In a May 1998 conference in Washington on U.S. media coverage of China shortly before President Clinton's visit to Beijing in late June, the Chinese participants argued that the U.S. news media have not been objective and constructive in their reporting of Sino-American relations. The American media were accused, in collaboration with the government, of demonizing China, creating barriers to a better understanding and relationship between the United States and China. Underpinning their accusation is the notion that the news media should not adversely affect U.S.-China relations and the friendship of the two peoples.

Such rhetoric was remarkably reminiscent of the language used by the Chinese Foreign Ministry in March 1961 after the negotiations for an exchange of correspondents between the two countries ground to a halt. The Beijing government insisted that any exchange of correspondents "must help eliminate estrangement between the Chinese and American peoples" and improve relations between the two nations. Because of clashing definitions of news and concepts of press freedom, after nearly four decades American news media still appear to be trapped in the high politics of U.S.-China relations.

HISTORICAL EXAMPLES ABOUND, especially during the years when actions of the governments of both the United States and China kept American reporters away from China. Following the Communist victory in China, the American media were hopelessly intertwined in U.S. national and international politics as Washington maneuvered to contain Beijing from all fronts. Expelled by Beijing and banned by Washington, the U.S. news media set up their posts in Hong Kong, Tokyo and other nearby Asian cities to monitor the revolutionary China through such Chinese media as Xinhua News Agency, *People's Daily, The Beijing Review* and Radio Beijing. With the U.S. media denied entry to China, other Western news agencies (Reuters and Agence France Presse, for example) filled in.

The proxy reporting undermined organizational autonomy and frustrated professional pride. The U.S. media deemed China too important to be left with either the specialists or non-Americans. For different reasons, China felt the same. In a surprise move in August 1956, Beijing invited 18 American reporters for a month's visit to see what the Chinese actually were doing. The move was more political than journalistic. The Beijing offer caught Washington off guard, causing the government to scramble for defense.

In response, both the State Department and the White House reiterated the U.S. travel ban on the grounds that China still held American prisoners from the Korean War. The American media organizations eventually declined the invitation, choosing instead to observe China from a distance defined and delimited by the U.S. policy. However, three journalists—Edmund Stevens and Philip Harrington from *Look* magazine and William Worthy from the *Baltimore Afro-American*—defied the ban and traveled to China in December 1956. Their trip prompted China to stress the idea of a reporters' exchange at the ambassadorial talks in Geneva. What Beijing sought in these discussions was not necessarily journalism in service of the public interest but some form of implicit American recognition of its status as a contending party in the China-Taiwan-U.S. triangular relationship. With its official title, the Republic of China, Taiwan still represented the whole China in the United States.

The Chinese proposal of a reporters' exchange prodded American journalism to take a higher journalistic moral stand and a practical appeal. In a February 7, 1957, editorial, *The New York Times* argued that "the American public is entitled to know from their own observers what is happening in Communist China. This is a question of freedom of the press and freedom of knowledge." *The Washington Post* later agreed in a June 25, 1957, editorial that "American coverage in Peking would open an invaluable window into Red China." The controversies surrounding the China travel ban led to a Senate Judiciary Constitutional Rights Subcommittee hearing in March 1957. Representatives from various major news organizations testified against the policy, arguing that it compromised American understanding of the fast-changing China. The government insisted that the ban stemmed from "fundamental United States foreign policy." In other words, restriction on China reporting was instrumental in U.S. isolation of China and rejection of the Communist regime's legitimacy. The Cold War between the two countries was obviously fought at the expense of the free flow of information in international communication.

Under pressure from news organizations, Congress and the public, the State Department in August 1957 finally gave approval to 24 reporters to visit China "in order to permit direct reporting by them to the American people about conditions in the area under Chinese Communist control." The policy shift clearly recognized basic journalistic canons: objectivity and the public's right to know. The U.S. permission was unilateral, however. China quickly rejected the U.S. decision as "completely unacceptable" and as "a typical expression of an imperialist government's attitudes." The talk of exchange of correspondents in Sino-American relations was disrupted by the second Taiwan Straits crisis in 1958 and ended two years later when Beijing was no longer interested in the issue. The rules of the game were put on hold.

In the early 1960s, the U.S. government made several attempts to resolve the impasse, including granting visas for Chinese reporters to come, but received no response from China. By 1966, although Washington had granted permission for more than 100 American correspondents to go to China, Beijing showed no sign of welcoming them. As China launched the Cultural Revolution and the United States plunged deeper into the Vietnam quagmire, the matter of reporters' exchange lost its currency and priority. For the American journalists, reporting China from behind the Bamboo Curtain thus represented not simply a standard journalistic procedure determined by functional prerequisites, but an unusual political privilege bound by national interests. On both counts, it remained a near impossibility. When other major Western countries had already established a beachhead in Beijing, most American correspondents continued to peek at China from the periphery. As close as it might be to China, Hong Kong could not convincingly measure the heartbeat of the country. The Beijing dispatches from Toronto's *Globe and Mail*, the only medium from North America in China at that time, provided a symbolic news link across the Pacific and a visible reminder of U.S. journalism's absence from China.

RELYING PRIMARILY ON indirect or alternative means, American news media managed to cover China's domestic affairs and the Communist postures toward the United States. Such off-the-spot journalistic practices invited criticism from China watchers, especially those who had visited Beijing. Supported by three trips to China before 1964, writer and filmmaker Felix Greene questioned "the accuracy of some of the reports about Communist China conveyed to the American people by the press." He believed that the misinformation in the U.S. press about Chinese contemporary political arrangements and social commitments contributed to the public's being "tragically ignorant" about China. A.T. Steele, a veteran China correspondent, dismissed Greene's accusation as "one-sided," but nevertheless admitted that China presented a tough problem for American correspondents since reliable information was hard to come by. Greene's critical challenge was rooted in a fundamental news conception: seeing is believing. He had been there in China and thus knew better.

For most American journalists who had never visited China, Greene's charges were difficult to refute. To deny there is no difference in the journalistic views between here and there is to accept the conceptual implausibility that our perspective of the world does not change according to where we may stand and what we perceive in it. After the rise of the Communists to power, China could not be unchanged or unchanging. Greene's unspoken empiricism of "being there" in China

observation raised serious epistemological and sociological issues—
the questions of reliability, sensitivity and validity—to the American
news media stranded "over here."

From 1957 to 1971, other than the ambassadorial talks in Geneva,
virtually no public communication channel was established between
China and the United States. Given their entanglement in the touchy
U.S.-China relations, whether the American news media had maintained an institutional independence in their China reporting was open
to debate. Using predominantly official policy statements and situation
analyses in the news, the U.S. media often saw China via the lens
specified by Washington's political calculation.

Governmental sources undoubtedly make the news. When the United
States and China kept a distance from each other, reporting China
inevitably followed the official Washington mode, particularly the
boundaries set by the White House. As sources of China related
events and issues, top officials from the executive branch dominated
the news. Congress turned out to be weak and ad hoc. Rarely did
nongovernmental voices emerge unless they appeared in an official
setting. In March 1966, during the Johnson presidency, the Senate
Foreign Relations Committee for the first time held monthlong hearings on a wide range of topics and options in U.S.-China policy. These
hearings were significant as national television exposed the American
public to a vivid debate over a country that all U.S. citizens were
barred from visiting.

Appearing before the Committee was a distinguished panel of China
scholars and experts: A. Doak Barnett, John K. Fairbank, Walter H.
Judd, Hans J. Morgenthau, Robert A. Scalapino and Benjamin I.
Schwartz. Most notable were Fairbank, a Harvard historian, and Barnett,
a political scientist at Columbia. Their China policy recommendations
struck a responsive chord among the U.S. news media. *The Washington Post* said in an editorial that Barnett and Fairbank "may not have
thought they were voicing original thoughts when they ventured their
approval of containment and their opposition to isolation." Their stat-
ure grew with time. Stanley Karnow in 1971 considered Fairbank as
"the most prominent American academic authority on China," followed by Barnett.

Fairbank's influences went beyond academic circles in China studies. He had been prominent in China reporting, first as a controversial
newsmaker during the debates over "Who lost China?" in the early

1950s and then as a persuasive news shaper in the 1960s. Both the *Times* and the *Post* highly regarded his vision and insights. Insightful and articulate as he was, however, Fairbank, like the other China specialists, could not claim firsthand knowledge about the country after 1950. As Stanley Karnow pointed out, "For all their expertise, most China specialists in government or in the universities lack a single vital credential—direct experience in China." He quoted an anonymous China expert as saying, "We've never felt the Chinese soil under our feet," implying lack of sensitivity to the traditions and customs that could only be acquired from "having been in the country." It was to these specialists whom journalists frequently turned for news and views about China in Sino-American relations.

It MIGHT BE ARGUED THAT, given the dearth of firsthand experience among the experts and journalists in the United States, it was the blind leading the blind in China reporting from 1950 through 1970. But this argument failed to realize that Sino-American politics was a product of international circumstances complicated by the rise of communism and its threats to democracy. The news media could only make out with what was possible and permissible in the larger environment. As A.T. Steele said, some American newspapers did "an outstanding job of covering China" to the extent that reliable information was available. That notwithstanding, for 20 years most information about China was generated in Washington and U.S. agencies overseas, not in Beijing. The implications are profound in news coverage of U.S.-China relations.

In a technical sense, most American reporters were grounded in Washington with no access to the other side of the U.S.-China equation. The structural constraints at the national level clearly favored the powers that be in the interplay between reporters and officials. It should be little surprise that China reporting echoed closely Washington's response to Beijing's domestic and foreign behaviors. As such, the political realities within and between China and the United States were mostly defined by foreign policy-makers. These definitions set the parameters within which the American news media functioned and performed their duties in China reporting. As the key agenda setter, the government was therefore likely to influence the scope and range of public understanding and debate of U.S.-China policy.

Either by design or by default, because of the exclusive nature of news gathering in Sino-American relations, a hierarchy of sources regulated the process of China reporting. When a small number of foreign policy-makers, such as the president, secretary of state and other top advisers, were given unrivaled access to the media, they were in a strategic position to manage the news through preplanned channels or leaks to control the flow and direction of information. Their dominant ideas and perspectives suggested a preferred reading in the news. In the short run, they helped perpetuate the hegemonic belief that foreign policy issues were beyond the realm of public participation. In the long run, they limited the range of options, solutions and actions presented to the public, thus affecting the stability and intensity of public opinion and its possible impact on official policy.

Not until the pingpong diplomacy in early 1971 when tensions between the two countries eased was a new page in Sino-American history opened. (It is no coincidence that, in line with the government's position, American public opinion remained opposed to Beijing's admission into the United Nations for 20 years until 1971.) For the first time since 1950, full-time U.S. professional journalists were able to enter China. Three reporters from the Associated Press and NBC in Tokyo observed the country in a close encounter.

THE THAW OF U.S.-CHINA RELATIONS picked up momentum, and American journalism went for an eye-opening and heart-pumping ride at the end. After a series of subtle political, secretive maneuvers by national security adviser Henry Kissinger, President Nixon shocked the whole world by announcing unexpectedly in 1971 that he would go to China. Under Nixon's instruction, the courtship of China would "be strictly secret," and the U.S. media had no inkling of the groundbreaking story. The closed politics, secrecy and news manipulation effectively sidestepped the U.S. media and brought them to their bended knees.

Nixon's historical trip in February 1972 sent 87 high-ranking U.S. media representatives to Beijing, which had refused to accept American journalists for 20 years. The long U.S. absence took its toll on the quality of China reporting. The sudden breakthrough in mass communication caught the press corps largely unprepared to deal with the land that, with all its ideological and sociocultural idiosyncrasies, had intrigued American journalism. China reporting, particularly on television, was not only inadequate but also superficial. As Newsweek put it, "One after another, live via satellite, the networks' brightest news stars popped up with hundred-year-old egg on their faces." If the on-site reporting was sub-par, the performance of off-shore American journalism became suspect when China was out of its reach during the '50s and '60s.

The opening of a window, albeit limited, was enough to get American news media excited about the opportunity to report from inside China. Max Frankel of *The New York Times* summed it up best in *Newsweek*: China "is still virgin territory as far as reporting is concerned. Every time you turn around there's something fresh and different and new." Frankel was neither naive nor ignorant. Like many others who had been cut off from China, he was simply too overwhelmed by the sights and sounds of the forbidden city. Getting back to China was just the beginning. Once there, American journalists needed to overcome many obstacles and difficulties in their China reporting. China was still very much a closed society, and the ideological and sociocultural differences between the two countries—not to mention the longstanding distrust and the incompatible media systems—were largely insurmountable.

During the years when China was closed to American reporters, the dependency of American journalists on sources in Washington and their exclusion from Beijing in China reporting represented a journalistic deference to governmental politics. At best, the unchallenged forum and uncontested news channels resulted in a simplistic and one-dimensional reality of Sino-American relations. At worst, the American journalists served as surrogate voices of the government, allowing it to control when, what and how other players and the public were to be involved in the decision-making process. Throughout the years, whether here in Washington or out there on the Chinese verge, given the reliance on official sources and the subsequent myopia, the independent character and professional integrity of American journalism became problematic. Without diversity and a wide-ranging spectrum of political messages in China reporting, the news media encouraged foreign policy-makers to draw the map of Sino-American relations in their own images and with their chosen configuration.

Tsan-Kuo Chang, an associate professor at the University of Minnesota-Twin Cities, is a former reporter and author of The Press and China Policy: The Illusion of Sino-American Relations, 1950-1984.

5

Chinese Media in Flux

From Party line to bottom line

Jaime A. FlorCruz

FOR SEVERAL MONTHS, THE FRIENDS of Nature, a Beijing-based environmental group, had been campaigning to save the Golden Monkey, which was disappearing along with its natural habitat, the virgin forests in southwestern Yunnan province. FON wrote letters to press Beijing's policy-makers to stop logging in Yunnan's Deqing County. In response, the central government ordered Deqing to quit logging, but the local government acceded only on condition that Beijing subsidize the loss of employment. Beijing pledged 11 million yuan (U.S.$1.33 million) yearly, and it seemed the Golden Monkey could escape extinction.

But when FON members revisited Deqing posing as investors, they found that logging continued. This time, they coaxed "Jiaodian Fangtan" ("Focal Point"), a 13-minute prime-time investigative newsmagazine broadcast daily by China Central Television (CCTV), to send a crew to document the deforestation. When the program aired August 2, the response was electric. Premier Zhu Rongji reportedly saw it and ordered Yunnan to stop logging immediately.

Such a positive outcome, although still uncommon, is emblematic of the growing power of the Chinese journalists. "Focal Point" has become must viewing for much of the country. Launched in April

1996, one-third of the programs are "critical," according to producer Jing Yidan. The show probes beyond the headlines, using legwork and man-on-the-street interviews to uncover riveting tales. Targets of exposés include corrupt local officials, enterprise managers, customs employees and tax collectors. An earlier "Focal Point" show, for example, exposed a case in which 400 pupils in Shanxian County in Shandong province were poisoned after taking fake iodine supplements. After watching the show, President Jiang Zemin phoned Ministry of Health and Shandong officials, ordering them to aid the sick pupils and punish the perpetrators. Song Xinhua, deputy director of the county's epidemic prevention station, it turned out, had promoted sales of iodine supplement pills in local schools for personal aggrandizement. Song was subsequently arrested.

This kind of muckraking approach has been responsible for the program's high ratings. Many leading officials are among "Focal Point's" avid viewers, including Premier Zhu Rongji, who says he watches the show almost every day. During a visit of CCTV in October 1998, Zhu encouraged TV journalists to work on more investigative reports and help strengthen the role of journalism as custodian of social conscience.

THE MEDIA'S NEWFOUND VIGOR would have been unthinkable only nine years ago. When the tanks of the People's Liberation Army crushed student protests in Tiananmen Square in June 1989, a decade of reform was left in shambles. In the wake of the crackdown, publications that showed "bourgeois liberal" tendencies were revamped by apparatchiks. Enterprising editors and reporters were sacked or sidelined. The press was muzzled, allowed only to churn out rosy propaganda. Freedom of expression became an empty slogan.

Despite the repression of the pro-democracy movement, however, continued market reform over the past decade has eroded the dominant position of the official media. As the media market continues to grow, the news media have become increasingly open and responsive to public demand. To the people in China, the press and broadcasters are now a real source of information and food for thought, rather than a skimpy compendium of sterile polemic and abstruse dogma. The vibrancy, diversity and enterprise of newspapers, magazines and television shows reflect growing pluralism—and Beijing's inability to control it.

Credit this sea change to two decades of market-oriented reforms. In the 1970s, during the reign of Chairman Mao Zedong, reporters—servants of the state—were admonished to love the *renmin*, the people, instead of simply seeking the truth. Now journalists, like everyone else in the People's Republic, are wont to love the *renminbi*—the people's currency. This change of orientation has revolutionized the media scene. National and local TV stations now offer infotainment fares like soap operas, sitcoms, music videos and reruns of "America's Funniest Home Video" and "Baywatch." Those in the market for serious topics may switch on to a slew of hard-hitting TV newsmagazines, like "Focal Point," "Frank Talk" and "Today's Topic," which touch on current events and social issues and run exposés of wrongdoings, corruption and malfeasance by officials. Nearly 2,000 newspapers are published across the country, competing for readership with 3,600 provincial, city and local papers. Thousands of magazines join them on the crowded newsstands.

Since China four years ago plugged into the yingtewang, as the Internet is known, more than 1.2 million Chinese have access to the Net, a number that is projected to grow to 5 million by 2000. Typically, these Netsurfers are young, single, well educated and relatively affluent—just the sort of person who might be inclined to question the Party line. The Internet is making it even harder for censors to control the flow of information. In cyberspace, after all, anyone with enough money to spend can be a publisher or propagandist. Recent trends point to increasing use of Chinese language on the Net, showing that even those who are not proficient in foreign languages can now tap into it. Despite limits on its use—the number of Chinese users are still a small percentage of the total population largely confined in the cities—the Internet is a liberating force.

THE MARKET-DRIVEN MEDIA BOOM has given rise to a new breed of journalists—younger, well traveled, better educated and less bound to political missions than profit or professional integrity. They run the media like enterprises, responsible for their profits and losses, and hold themselves answerable to readers and advertisers. Increasingly, it is the market, not the Communist Party, that drives the media. Publishers think not only in terms of politics, but of advertising, making them more responsive to their audience's changing tastes and expectations. Under their aegis, the Chinese press has begun to redefine its role: one

recent survey found that 70 percent of journalists ranked social re-
sponsibility as their top priority, while only 27.5 percent felt they
should serve as mouthpieces of the Party.

A surge in investigative reporting caters to a large audience rankled
by petty and large-scale corruption. The Guangzhou-based *Nanfang
Zhoumo* (*Southern Weekend*) has doubled its circulation to 1.3 million
since 1992 by specializing in front-page exposés of social ills. Recent
topics touched on prickly issues like the resettlement of people displaced by the Three Gorges dam project, violations of workers' rights
and police abuse.

The press has not totally shed its role as Big Brother. Muckraking
also serves the interests of Beijing, where officials fear that unchecked
graft and corruption could spark social unrest. Carefully calibrated
exposés serve as social safety valves that release a catharsis of pent-up
frustrations. The targets of these exposés are often chosen as much for
their political vulnerability as for the blatant nature of their abuses.
Nevertheless, the masses respond positively to such crusades. They
write or phone in complaints and praises. Most exposés target erring
petty officials and ordinary citizens. The "big tigers"—like Chen Xitong,
a former mayor and party chief of Beijing who was recently convicted
of graft charges—are hunted down only when it suits the political
agenda of more powerful figures. Direct criticisms of those top officials remain taboo. Nevertheless, even if these investigations and arrests are set up, ordinary people, as well as officials on all levels, are
becoming more and more sensitized to the concept of accountability
before the law. The Party is undermining its authority.

DIVERSE FORCES ARE PAVING THE way for a freer press. Government
subsidies to state-run media institutions are drying up quickly. Xinhua's
subsidy is said to be dwindling at 7 percent yearly. Smaller publications, such as the magazine *Tiyu Huabao* (*China Sports*), last year
were given a time limit to turn profits, find a foreign partner or fold
up, because the government was stopping its handouts. Incipient com-
mercialism is eroding the traditional supremacy of the state media.
Very few people read them; even fewer subscribe to them. *The People's
Daily*, the Communist Party's flagship paper, which cornered a circulation of nearly 7 million at the start of Deng Xiaoping's economic
reforms in 1979, now has only 2 million. Meanwhile, the Shanghai-
based *Xinmin Evening Daily*, which specializes in pithy, colorful

infotainment, boasts of a daily circulation of 1.7 million—and bulging advertising revenues. Nearly 100 other evening papers, their editors still chosen by the Party, have mushroomed to emulate that formula.

Communist Party publications are now fighting for survival in this reform-or-perish milieu. During the secretive years under Chairman Mao, the *Cankao Xiaoxi* (*Reference News*), a daily compilation of translated foreign news, used to be restricted to Chinese readers. Now it is sold openly and available by subscription. No wonder: its subscription has dwindled from 7 million in the 1970s to 2 million today. *People's Daily* has introduced a four-page financial section, featuring regular candlestick charts for the Shanghai and Shenzhen composite stock indices, to cater to the more than 32 million Chinese who now play the stock market. Even the stodgy Xinhua News Agency has diversified into the lucrative public relations and financial data business.

Such grudging capitulation testifies to the changing tastes and increased savvy of the consumers of news. To gain credibility and expand its audience, these state media now look to improve the speed and accuracy of their reporting. Once they could ignore or cover up natural or man-made disasters. Now they swiftly report even "negative" subjects like the recent bombings in Beijing and Urumqi, the earthquakes in Kunming and the flooding along the Yangzi River.

But the tyranny of the market has also spawned abuses. Obsession with the bottom line has sometimes prompted reckless reporting and mercenary practices. Infomercials are passed off as news articles. Journalists often ask publicists for "taxi fare"—cash bribes—to ensure positive coverage. Glossy magazines and racy tabloids feature sexy pinups and salacious tales of sex and violence to pander to more prurient tastes. The centuries-old classic "The Water Margin" was recently reissued under the title "Three Women and 105 Men." "The Lives of Marx, Engels, Lenin and Stalin" reappeared as "The Four Most Attractive Men."

This new freedom remains under constant threat from Party apparatchiks, like conservative Minister of Propaganda Ding Guangen, who expects journalists to "stay loyal to socialism." Beijing's leaders have no intention of unleashing a totally free press. The unspoken threat of punishments—fines, reprimands, even prison terms—create a chilling effect of self-censorship that is planted in the journalist's subconscious. Indeed, several Chinese journalists who have allegedly breached opaque taboos—like Gao Yu, a free-lancer writing about political issues for the Hong Kong-based magazine *Jing Bao* (*The Mirror*)—are languishing in mainland prisons.

Still, despite the vestigial influence of the Communist apparatchiks, people in China now have unprecedented access to the benefits, as well as excesses, of a pluralistic, competitive media market. Change is in the offing, and everyone hopes to know about it through the media.

Jaime A. FlorCruz is the Beijing bureau chief for Time *magazine.*

Part 2

COMMUNICATING

Amid pious invocations of multiculturalism, a shrinking world and the imminent arrival of the Pacific Century, the peoples of Asia and the West continue to view each other through veils of cliché and misunderstanding. —PETER CONN

6

Pearl S. Buck

*For two generations of Americans, as an author
and journalist, Buck invented China.*

Peter Conn

PEARL BUCK WAS, AS HISTORIAN James Thomson noted, "the most influential Westerner to write about China since 13th-century Marco Polo." Thomson's assessment is at once indisputable, familiar, and yet, upon reflection, astonishing. Never before or since has one writer so personally shaped the imaginative terms in which America addresses a foreign culture. For two generations of Americans, Buck invented China.

She wrote more than 70 books, many of them best sellers, including 15 Book-of-the-Month Club selections. She worked in virtually every genre of writing, including novels, short stories, plays, biography, autobiography, translations (from the Chinese), children's literature, essays, poetry. However steeply she has fallen from critical favor, she had in fact won the Nobel Prize in literature (with Toni Morrison, she is one of only two American women ever to do so), and a Pulitzer, and the Howells Medal, and election to the National Academy and Institute of Arts and Letters, and a dozen honorary degrees.

And she was a journalist. From the '30s into the '50s, when the bedrock of her status as America's best-known authority on Asia rested on her being author of the novel *The Good Earth*, she also reached people on a wide range of topics in newspapers and magazines. She

43

tirelessly set her ideas on Asia, civil rights, women and more before the American public in publications as varied as *Harper's Magazine, Saturday Review, The New York Times Magazine, Life*, the Urban League's *Opportunity, The New York Herald Tribune's Book Review*, the National Association for the Advancement of Colored People's *Crisis* and *Modern Maturity*. With her husband, Richard Walsh, she published the magazine Asia, which for a time had a substantial influence on American opinion about East Asia. She wrote books of topical nonfiction, such as *Of Women and Men*, a tough-minded survey of relations between the sexes on the eve of American entry into World War II, *American Unity and Asia*, a collection of her articles and speeches on civil rights and international politics, and *Friend to Friend*, a conversation with Carlos P. Romulo, the foreign minister of the Philippines, which dealt frankly with conflicts between Americans and Asians. She also applied her knowledge of journalism in her novel *God's Men*: the book, which appeared after Buck's friendship with Henry Luce snapped over his support for Chiang Kai-shek, pilloried a character who closely resembled the publisher.

Buck's stories of China were based on her own experiences and observations as a missionary daughter. Her parents were an ill-matched pair of Southern Presbyterians named Absalom and Carie Sydenstricker. Pearl was born in West Virginia, while her parents were on a home leave, but she was taken to China at three months old and lived there for most of the next 40 years. She grew up bilingual, speaking and reading both English and Chinese. In her own favorite metaphor, she described herself as "culturally bifocal." At the same time, from her earliest days, she felt herself homeless in both her countries, an outsider among people different from herself.

Unlike almost every other American of her generation, Pearl Buck grew up knowing China as her actual day-to-day world, while America was the place of conjecture and simplified images. Furthermore, almost uniquely among white American writers, she spent the first half of her life as a minority person, an experience that had much to do with her lifelong passion for interracial understanding.

She went to college in the United States, at Randolph-Macon Woman's College in Virginia but returned to China immediately after graduation. Shortly after going back to China, she married her first husband, the agricultural economist J. Lossing Buck, and began a family. For several years, the couple lived in the town of Nanxuzhou

(Nanhsuchou) in rural Anhui (Anhwei) province. Buck published her first stories and novels, including *The Good Earth* in 1931, while still living in China.

In the early 1930s, with China torn by civil war, Japanese invasions and mounting anti-foreign violence, she moved to the United States, buying a dilapidated 18th-century farmhouse in Bucks County, north of Philadelphia. The place was called Green Hills Farm, and it served as home and headquarters for several decades of activity. Here she continued to write, to raise the seven children she adopted and to manage the various organizations she founded to address the problems of ethnic hatred and to help displaced and disadvantaged children.

She wrote steadily during her first American years, mainly nonfiction and occasional stories. Many of her essays and book reviews appeared in *Asia*, where she was increasingly active as an editor and contributor. After war broke out in Asia, she devoted even more of her writing to political subjects. In rapid succession, she published a series of six articles in *Asia*, commenting on such subjects as military tactics, American neutrality and the political background of the struggle. *Asia* also published essays by Edgar Snow, which evolved into his landmark book *Red Star Over China*, a history of Chinese communism grounded in Snow's interviews with Mao Zedong at his headquarters in Yenan. Buck, who loathed communism, recognized that the strength of Chinese communism was its character as a peasant movement that had awakened the common people as no other. At the same time, she was severely critical of Chiang Kai-shek and his Nationalists, whom she saw as both corrupt and murderous.

In an article in *Asia* in 1939, Buck pointed out that the war in Asia involved more people and a larger territory than the conflict in Europe. Americans remained generally indifferent, though, to events on the other side of the Pacific. Throughout her American years, Pearl Buck was one of the leading figures in the effort to promote cross-cultural understanding between Asia and the United States. In the pages of Asia, she encouraged articles and stories from Asian writers, including Jawaharlal Nehru, Mao Zedong and Soong Qingling (Sun Yat-sen's widow).

She also committed the pages of *Asia* to exposing the contradiction between the United States and Britain's opposition to fascism and their own flawed conduct with regard to people of color—specifically, the Jim Crow system in the United States and Britain's colonial domination of India. "To fight with England for Europe's freedom while India is governed by tyranny, is a monstrous contradiction, and yet no more monstrous than that while the United States prepares for a mighty defense of her democracy twelve million Americans should be denied equality in a nation founded upon equal opportunity for all."

Once the United States entered the war, she did not mince words when she saw wrong. In the summer of 1942 she published a collection of her articles and speeches on civil rights and international politics in a book titled *American Unity and Asia*. Along with several statements on the status
of African-Americans and women, Buck rather bravely included a speech she had made condemning the internment of Japanese-Americans. With that speech, she joined a small handful of white Americans who opposed one of the most shameful domestic proceedings of World War II. In 1943, she published an article in *The New York Times Magazine* scolding the Allies for failing to include universal human equality among their war aims.

For part of the war, Buck maintained a disapproving silence on America's ally Chiang Kai-shek. When she finally decided to speak out, she chose the most visible journal in America: she asked Henry Luce to publish a moderate but critical estimate of Chiang in *Life*. It proved to be one of the most important articles she ever wrote.

After some considerable hesitation, Luce agreed to publish the article, under the title "A Warning About China." Buck argued that Chiang was still regarded in China as a great military figure, but that he was losing support through his ruthless suppression of liberal voices. His success, indeed his survival, would depend upon reforms within the Guomindang and within his innermost circle. Buck called for greater American assistance, but she also placed much of the blame for the failures of Chiang's leadership squarely with Chiang himself.

To Luce's credit, he published Buck's article in spite of his violent disagreement with it. As he predicted, "A Warning About China" helped to swing American opinion away from Chiang. Looking back on Chinese-American relations in that period, John King Fairbank later wrote: "American disillusionment as to Free China came with a bang in the summer of 1943 through three articles—Pearl Buck in *Life* for May 10, Hanson Baldwin of *The New York Times* in the *Reader's Digest* for August, and T.A. Bisson in *Far Eastern Survey*."

Buck's criticisms of Chiang led to the charge that she was disloyal.

Six years later, in June 1949, with the Japanese defeated and the Chinese civil war grinding toward a Communist victory, she found herself sharing a front-page story in the *New York Sun* with a long list of other celebrities who had been named as "Red appeasers" by a California state legislator. According to Sen. Jack Tenney, Pearl had "conspicuously followed or appeased some of the Communist Party line over a long period of time," and so had Charles Chaplin, Helen Gahagan Douglas, Langston Hughes, Danny Kaye, Gene Kelly, Thomas Mann, Frederic March, Burgess Meredith, Dorothy Parker, Gregory Peck, Vincent Price, Paul Robeson, Edward G. Robinson, Artie Shaw, Frank Sinatra and Orson Welles, among many others.

Pearl issued a denial, part of which was quoted in *The New York Times*. "I am anti-Communist," she said, "to the last drop of my blood." At the same time, she condemned the California report as undemocratic, and—in sentences the *Times* chose not to quote—she warned that anti-Communist excesses were "making our country a laughing stock for the whole world." To our foreign allies and adversaries alike, we seemed to be "a nation of fools."

In a season of hysteria, Pearl tried to restore a measure of balance. In late October 1949, just a few weeks after Mao had installed himself in Beijing, she published a long article, "Our Dangerous Myths About China," in *The New York Times Magazine*. Americans, she said, stored "an amazing amount of trash in our mental attics when it comes to the Chinese," including the stereotype, "old and cobwebby indeed," that the Chinese are "mysterious and inscrutable." Displaying considerable courage, she attempted to puncture another myth: the belief that "all those who now proceed under the Communist banner are evil men."

She made a number of predictions about China's probable course under the Communists. History confirmed her judgment that "collective farms go against [the Chinese] grain," and that collectivized farming would fail. On the other hand, she underestimated Mao's demagogic powers. Mao would never hypnotize his people, Pearl said, because "the sort of ecstasy into which the German people seem to have fallen before a man in a uniform, shouting among flags, is impossible to a people as long sane as the Chinese." On the contrary, Mao would soon become the center of the 20th-century's most hysterical cult of personality, presiding over decades of insanity whose victims would be numbered in the millions.

If Buck's prominence as an American expert on China faded in the

1950s, she remained active on the issues of race, women and children's welfare. In 1950, Buck published a book called *The Child Who Never Grew*, a story about her retarded daughter, Carol. The book was a landmark. Specifically, it encouraged Rose Kennedy to talk publicly about her retarded child, Rosemary. More generally, it helped to change American attitudes toward mental illness. Nevertheless, there is no avoiding the fact that she faded from public knowledge.

How does a woman of this magnitude and range slip away from our national consciousness? She has not exactly disappeared. Rather, as one observer shrewdly put it, she has been "hidden in plain sight," obscured beneath a caricature that belies her complexity and her achievement. She has become a durable, one-woman punch line, trapped in some version or other of the old joke, "If Pearl Buck is the answer, then what is the question?"

In the years after World War II, Buck's literary reputation shrank to the vanishing point. She stood on the wrong side of virtually every line drawn by those who constructed the lists of required reading in the 1950s and 1960s. To begin with, her principal subjects were women and China, both of which were regarded as peripheral and even frivolous in the early postwar years. Academics were then manufacturing the new field of "American Studies," and devising reading lists and courses that would allegedly document the "American character" or the "American mind" or "American identity." As far as they were concerned, neither Pearl Buck nor Asian culture had any contribution to make to their grand but ultimately myopic enterprise. Furthermore, she preferred episodic plots to complex structures and had little interest in psychological analysis. In addition to all that, she was not a felicitous stylist, and she even displayed a taste for formulaic phrases. Needless to say, none of this endeared her to that vast cultural heartland stretching from the East River to the Hudson.

She was also the victim of political hostility, attacked by the right for her active civil rights efforts, distrusted by the left because of her vocal anti-communism. Beyond that, she undoubtedly suffered because of her gender: more often than not, it was her male rivals and critics who declared that her gigantic success only demonstrated the bad judgment of American readers—especially women readers, who have always made up the majority of Buck's audience.

The warming of relations between the United States and China seemed to offer her an opportunity to resume contact with the country that was her first home. She became increasingly absorbed with the idea of returning to China before she died and made numerous efforts to accompany Richard Nixon as a journalist when he made his journey to China in February 1972. The Chinese government, however, rejected her request for a visa. In May 1972, after months of official silence, a Chinese envoy stationed in Canada sent her a terse, brutal message:

> Dear Miss Pearl Buck:
> Your letters have been duly received. In view of the fact that for a long time you have in your works taken an attitude of distortion, smear and vilification towards the people of new China and its leaders, I am authorized to inform you that we cannot accept your request for a visit to China.

Early in the morning of March 6, 1973, after a quiet night, she died. The cause of death was lung cancer. Newspapers around the world covered Pearl's death as a front-page story. *The New York Times* ran a 3,000-word obituary by Albin Krebs; an appraisal, under the headline A MISSIONARY HERITAGE by Thomas Lask; and a flattering editorial. Even Pearl's old adversaries at Time magazine, after reassuring their readers that she "was anything but a great novelist," made a few kind noises. President Nixon eulogized her as a "bridge between the civilizations of the East and West."

In the past couple of years, there have also been a few signs of renewed interest in Pearl Buck in the United States and Europe. In the spring of 1992, Buck's 100th birthday was marked by a major symposium at Randolph-Macon Woman's College, and the papers from that event have recently been published. In 1993, public television broadcast a widely applauded biography of Buck, called "East Wind, West Wind." More recently, Buck was the subject of a documentary on Belgian national radio. Perhaps, somewhat belatedly, this remarkable woman is being restored to a measure of greater visibility on both sides of the world.

In 1992, the Chinese-American writer Maxine Hong Kingston saluted Buck for making Asian voices heard, for the first time, in Western literature. By representing Chinese characters with "such empathy and compassion," Kingston said, Buck "was translating my parents to me and she was giving me our ancestry and our habitation." More recently, Toni Morrison looked back on her early reading of Buck's novels and said, with affectionate irony: "She misled me . . . and made me feel that all writers wrote sympathetically, empathetically, honestly and forthrightly about other cultures."

Americans have fought three Asian wars in the last 50 years. More recently, armed combat has been followed by economic competition: since the late 1970s, a half-dozen Asian nations have been the sites of unprecedented development in manufacturing and trade. In addition, within the United States itself, Asians make up the fastest-growing ethnic populations; Asian and Asian-American immigrants and native-born citizens now number more than 6 million people, a doubling in 10 years. Americans are beginning to realize that their future is entangled with Asia.

Nevertheless, amid pious invocations of multiculturalism, a shrinking world and the imminent arrival of the Pacific Century, the peoples of Asia and the West continue to view each other through veils of cliché and misunderstanding. At such a moment in political and cultural history, Pearl Buck's work should be a subject of increasing relevance and even urgency. Whatever the strengths or limits of her Asian images, she was a pioneer, introducing American readers to landscapes and people they had long ignored.

Peter Conn holds the Andrea Mitchell Chair in English at the University of Pennsylvania. This essay is adapted from his book, Pearl S. Buck: A Cultural Biography *(Cambridge University Press, 1996).*

7

Beyond the Square

Media treatment of China after Tiananmen

Carolyn Wakeman

As the 10th anniversary of mass demonstrations in Tiananmen Square approaches, reminders of the brutal suppression that followed weeks of peaceful protest in Beijing only intermittently shape news stories about China. Many American reporters in 1998 cover not only the government's efforts to avert economic crisis but also social trends, cultural events, even legal, military and political developments, without reference to the army's assault on unarmed civilians in the streets of the capital. A recent series in *The New York Times*, for example, examined the impact of environmental regulations, the spread of urban poverty, the persistence of women's inequality and the moderation of family planning policy without allusion to the events in Tiananmen. The omission signals recognition that China has changed dramatically since 1989, as well as a growing convergence of editorial sentiment with foreign policy, or at least a grudging acceptance of the Clinton strategy of "constructive engagement."

Any mention of Beijing's vast central square can, of course, still trigger memories of the bloodshed, as when an October 10, 1998 story in *The New York Times* about China's first Hollywood-style movie premiere stated that "the crowd of mostly young Beijingers filed in from the misty night off Tiananmen Square." But in recent weeks only the Times' report on October 28 about political tightening in late October referred specifically to the 1989 repression, and then in the context of describing gradual change: "Over all, the climate for open discussion is somewhat looser than it was during the previous nine years, since the violent crackdown on demonstrators in 1989." Even a November 9, 1998, report from Lhasa, explaining enduring hopes for the Dalai Lama's return, relinquished an opportunity to recall Tiananmen, stating that "the political atmosphere in China seems more open to negotiations on Tibet than at any time in a decade." Reminders of China's ruthless state control nearly a decade ago, especially for reporters based in Beijing and Shanghai who observe moderating trends, are no longer routine.

To be sure, other media voices, primarily based in the United States, have not relented, particularly when remembrance advances political interests and agendas. President Clinton's visit to China in July occasioned renewed allegations about the Tiananmen massacre, with critics deriding the announcement of a protocol appearance in the Square as craven and unprincipled, calling the welcoming ceremony, as *Newsweek* put it June 29, 1998, "just a kowtow to a tyrant." Administration officials nevertheless sought to substitute diplomacy for symbolism, hoping that "this nine-day trip would, by pointing up positive changes since the 1989 Tiananmen Square massacre, promote what a senior State Department official called 'the de-demonization of China,'" as *Time* reported June 6, 1998. A number of editors declined that message, alert to the still powerful resonance and widespread appeal of the Square as killing field.

UNLIKE REPORTERS based in Beijing, hard-liners in the press and in Congress continue to see China as essentially unchanged, columnist Jonathan Alter commented in *Newsweek*, July 6, 1998. They envision "a gulag of forced labor, constant repression and a small corps of brave dissidents battling a closed society." *Newsday*'s Asia correspondent Dele Olojede, on June 28, 1998, also noted a perception gap: "Listening to the Washington drumbeat of criticism that only grew louder as Clinton prepared his visit, there were few places on earth more infernal than China. Congressional leaders from both parties increasingly called for Clinton to cancel the trip outright or at least snub his hosts by boycotting welcoming ceremonies scheduled for Tiananmen Square. By their reckoning, China practices widespread repression, forced abortion is commonplace, the jails teem with democracy advocates and Tiananmen, almost literally speaking, still runs red with students' blood." Those assumptions fuel outrage.

A surge of China criticism in 1997 demonstrated the vigor of hardline views, urging expressions of protest, trade sanctions or containment, warning that Beijing poses not only a human rights threat to its own people but a serious military threat to the rest of Asia, even to the United States. That argument received its most forceful articulation in Richard Bernstein and Ross Munro's book *The Coming Conflict with China*, which sparked a flurry of media debate about U.S.-China policy. Also last year, on the eve of Jiang Zemin's visit to Washington, former Reagan National Security Council aide Oliver L. North suggested the civilian reach of the China threat in an October 28 *New York Times* article: "'I think there's an increasing awareness of the broad spectrum of threat Communist China poses to the American workers, to our environment, to the human rights ideals this country has stood for for more than two centuries.'" Staunch human rights advocates like San Francisco Rep. Nancy Pelosi objected fiercely to Jiang's ceremonial reception in Washington. As the *San Francisco Chronicle* wrote October 28, 1998: "For the president to be rolling out the red carpet for the head of a regime that has slaughtered its children in Tiananmen Square ... is totally inappropriate." Such assertions attracted press attention, keeping notions of China's menace and its ruthlessness potent.

Even though China-based correspondents no longer refer to a "Tiananmen Square massacre," an installment of "Twentieth Century" aired in October 1998 reinforced that image for television audiences. Host Mike Wallace announced that his program would show how events in China during mid-May 1989 "led to the massacre in Tiananmen Square." Once again compelling footage of the June 4 violence captured the murderous automatic weapons fire of the PLA, the defiant response of rock-throwing crowds, the overturned buses and burning personnel carriers, the blood streaked victims and the often replayed sequence of a solitary figure stopping a line of tanks. Noting that the Chinese have still "refused to apologize for the massacre in Tiananmen Square," the TV documentary gave powerful reiteration to a familiar story.

The problem, according to Jay Mathews, *The Washington Post*'s former bureau chief in Beijing, is that no corroborated eyewitness account documents either a massacre or the slaughter of students on

June 4 in Tiananmen. "Hundreds of people, most of them workers and passersby, did die on that night," Mathews wrote in the September 1998 *Columbia Journalism Review*, "but in a different place and under different circumstances." Beijing's streets, but not the Square itself, were stained with blood. And, Mathews insists, accuracy matters. Since the American press has often demanded that the Chinese government reveal the truth about Tiananmen, reporters cannot themselves endorse a myth and perpetuate a falsehood.

Human Rights Watch researcher Robin Munro, one of the last to leave the Square in the early morning of June 4, had long ago urged the foreign press to rely on fact rather than rumor and assumption. His detailed cross-referencing of conflicting, often exaggerated testimony led him to conclude in *The Nation* on June 11, 1990, that "several dozen people died in the immediate environs of the square and a few in the square itself. But to speak of that as the real massacre distorts the citywide nature of the carnage and diminishes the real political drama that unfolded in Tiananmen Square." If left uncorrected, such faulty reporting would shape the historical record, Munro feared, and "forever distort the future course of events." Moreover, Western criticisms based on a false version of the clearing of Tiananmen Square handed the Beijing authorities an unnecessary propaganda coup both at home and abroad, validating their claim of American press distortion.

THE PHRASE "TIANANMEN SQUARE MASSACRE" remains a kind of shorthand for everything that happened in China in 1989, remarked Richard Gordon, co-director of the award-winning documentary film *The Gate of Heavenly Peace*, at a recent conference held at the Graduate School of Journalism at the University of California, Berkeley. After all the saturation television coverage, when the three major networks broadcast more news about China in four months than over the previous 10 years, what people have retained is an impression of events that didn't happen. "Reporters created a kind of epic story that showed good pitted against evil, young against old, freedom against totalitarianism," Gordon observed. Historians like Joseph Esherick have also argued that the term "democracy movement" has often obscured rather than explained a complicated and highly theatrical series of events in 1989. Prevailing media opinion, nevertheless, remained for much of the decade largely content with a familiar simplification.

Deeply shaken by the slaughter of innocents whose cause had for weeks drawn their support, reporters who witnessed the bloodshed and interviewed survivors understandably found a simplified narrative irresistible. The dramatic story of heroic students prepared to sacrifice their lives for American freedoms validated the deepest cultural assumptions and most cherished political values of reporters and editors. It appealed to broad media audiences never before interested in China. With communism fallen in Eastern Europe, the televised spectacle of a massive outpouring of popular opposition to Party control in Beijing had sparked American hopes that somehow impassioned students quoting "Give me liberty or give me death" in English presaged the downfall of the Chinese government. The bold erection of the Goddess of Democracy statue in Tiananmen Square seemed a jubilant triumph rather than a foolhardy provocation. Disappointment heightened outrage.

Western correspondents took leave of their customary cynicism to romanticize the "democracy movement," Amanda Bennett contended in the *Wall Street Journal.* They became "emotionally involved with the Chinese students, their cause, their rhetoric, their marches, their innocence, and their aspirations—sometimes to the detriment of accurate and objective reporting." Reporters also began to believe that their urgent dispatches would reinforce and protect the demonstrators while assisting the victory of democracy over totalitarianism. Inevitably they felt "jilted," as historian James Thomson has remarked, when the crackdown and ensuing bloodshed brought a cruel and disillusioning end to their expectations.

Why did the China story provoke such an intense reaction, especially in the United States, sociologist Richard Madsen has asked. After all, on the weekend of June 4, three other major events occurred, each with potentially greater implications for Americans than the bloodshed in Beijing. Iran's Ayatollah Khomeini died, the Solidarity movement won a landslide victory in Poland's first free elections, and scandal forced the resignation of Speaker of the House Jim Wright. Madsen contends that the Tiananmen Square drama, at least as presented by the major news media, resonated with America's central myths. As NBC News anchor Tom Brokaw attested, Tiananmen "penetrated the American consciousness."

THE KILLING OF STUDENTS ABROAD does not always arouse such a sustained outpouring of anger and sympathy. The American media paid far less attention to the brutal suppression of demonstrations in 1980 by the South Korean government. Even though reporters for several newspapers in Seoul walked off their jobs to protest press censorship, and in Kwangju the army killed some 100 students protesting martial law and demanding direct popular election of the president, that slaughter failed to trigger widespread outrage in the United States. Media reports called the 200,000 demonstrators "insurgents" and "militants," stating that some of them remained "still at large" after the army's brutal crackdown. U.S. officials said they would continue to press the South Koreans for liberalization, but neither they nor the press nor the public demanded sanctions or reprisals.

Restraint also characterized American reporting on South Korea during nine days of fiery protests in 1996. Hundreds of students were injured and more than 5,000 detained for demanding the right to meet with North Korean counterparts in a border village, but government repression again aroused little American fervor. South Korean students were seen more as a threat to social order in a democratizing country than as courageous opponents of authoritarian repression. Tiananmen was different, and the roots of that difference lie in the history of American visions of China. For more than a century Americans have oscillated between seeing the Chinese as noble peasants and Oriental demons. Missionaries, businessmen, the military and journalists have each contributed different elements to the picture of China that has emerged in the United States.

THE AMERICAN GOAL OF CHANGING China through benevolent intervention began more than a century ago when missionaries journeyed across the Pacific to lift a benighted people out of darkness and "save China for Christ." Moral objectives accompanied burgeoning commercial interests as well, lending sanction to the British-American Tobacco Co.'s promotion of American cigarettes in China as a harmless substitute for an opium-addicted populace. Hollywood reflected popular sentiments in 1935 when the film "Oil for the Lamps of China" ascribed laudable motives to Standard Oil employees "sent out to China to dispel the darkness of centuries with the light of a new era." Their more immediate purpose was selling American oil, but sentiment and incentive overlapped. Faith, profit and patriotism all supported the noble, indeed responsible, goal of converting the heathen and capitalizing on the

"China market," efforts that required American gunboats to guard the treaty ports, patrol the rivers and protect inland mission stations from potentially hostile hordes.

The prospect of 450 million consumers eager to purchase American products never materialized, but a belief in the potential of the China trade persisted. "During most of the 19th and 20th centuries," notes historian Michael Schaller, "American trade with China remained at a low level, fluctuating between 1 percent and 2 percent of the total volume of exports." Missionary efforts accomplished similarly modest gains, and "not more than 1 percent of the Chinese people ever converted." But failure never extinguished hope. Capitalism and Christianity remained righteous causes, with setbacks inevitable but ultimate victory assured. Disappointment bred resentment.

Projections of fantasy and fear onto China were well established by the 1930s and 1940s, argued a startling Frontline "Special Report," called "Misunderstanding China," aired in 1972 on the eve of President Nixon's historic visit. The special documented for television viewers the stereotypical images of good and bad Chinese that defined American attitudes. Pulp magazines captivated readers with sinister villains like Fu Manchu. Hollywood films depicted Chinese warlords and Boxer zealots as menacing, cruel and cunning, requiring foreign suppression within their own borders, while a noble and long-suffering populace awaited deliverance from ignorance, oppression, poverty and disease. Favorite film stars like Ingrid Bergman and Humphrey Bogart set out on the silver screen to rescue China from its backwardness and free its people from evil overlords, providing affecting drama and also mirroring audience assumptions.

Those polarized distinctions gathered impetus during America's World War II alliance with Nationalist China against Japan. Theodore White and others in the Chongqing-based foreign press corps reported on Nationalist press censorship and forced conscription, endemic corruption and the brutal repression of domestic critics. American journalists who traveled to the guerrillas' headquarters in Yenan described Communist leaders as patriots resisting Japan and as populists far more likely to support democratic reforms than the central government. For most Americans, however, Nationalists and Communists remained polar opposites—China's civil war from 1946 to 1949 a clear-cut struggle between good and evil. Once Winston Churchill declared in 1946 that an "iron curtain" had fallen over Europe, jeopardizing the free world, the fear of Chinese communism gathered urgency.

When extended American military aid to the Nationalists failed to prevent a Communist victory, disappointment at the "loss" of China stirred denunciation. The engagement of American troops in Korea a year later in the effort to contain communism's advance amplified the impression of all "red" Chinese as sinister, or at least as hopelessly brainwashed by political commissars directed from the Soviet Union. Good Chinese had fled Communist rule to establish the Republic of China in Taiwan. Not only did the press in 1959 label the Chinese government "the most totalitarian regime of the 20th century," anthropologist Steven Mosher notes, but a 1965 Gallup poll querying Americans about the nation they liked least showed China at the bottom of a list of 28 countries.

To garner public support for the 1972 state visit, the Nixon administration enlisted the media in moderating hostile judgments. Journalists granted a glimpse behind the Bamboo Curtain described the order and cleanliness of China's cities, the prosperity and contentment of its peasants, the magnanimity of selfless officials who served the people. Denied unsupervised contact with ordinary citizens, they minimized the devastation of the Cultural Revolution. A less demonizing look at China from afar prepared the way for the normalization of Sino-American relations seven years later, and by 1980 scholarly exchanges had fostered growing interest in an opening China. American news bureaus located in Beijing, exotic tourism blossomed and the anticipation of a lucrative China market revived. The bad leaders of the revolutionary decades seemed replaced by good leaders like Deng Xiaoping, himself a victim of the Cultural Revolution, his personal experience of political persecution reinforcing his pragmatic belief in the necessity for openness and modernization. *Time* named Deng "Man of the Year" in 1978.

Throughout the 1980s, journalists continued to report that China had a "dark side," that although the government had pronounced getting rich to be glorious, it still punished dissent and mounted campaigns against "spiritual pollution" and "bourgeois liberalization." A Gallup poll nevertheless revealed that 72 percent of Americans in May of 1989 held a favorable opinion of China. A nation once consigned irrevocably to the Soviet camp was expressing keen interest in notions of democracy and representative government, setting up university programs in American studies and stocking libraries with donated American books, embracing Western mores, clothing styles, movies, popular music and fast food.

The brutal crackdown in 1989 caused poll numbers to shift dramatically and 78 percent of Americans to view China with disfavor. The country's leaders were perceived as butchers, the Communist Party as malevolent, the Chinese people as helpless victims, confirming prior American assumptions. Juxtaposed images of bad leaders suppressing good citizens became commonplace in the 1990s. Such judgments received powerful elaboration in *China Wakes*, the book that emerged in 1994 from Pulitzer Prize-winning journalists Nicholas Kristof and Sheryl WuDunn's experiences covering China for *The New York Times* from 1988 to 1993.

Kristof and WuDunn intersperse accounts of the 1989 demonstrations and the ongoing political repression with descriptions of an extraordinary rise in living standards and the varied achievements of a rapidly developing economy. "As living standards soar, it becomes increasingly dizzying to try to reconcile the two faces of China," they contend. "The important thing is to recognize the reality of both dimensions of China, to acknowledge that the government represses the people at the same time that it allows them to emerge from polio and poverty." Such attempts in the mid-1990s to reconcile two dimensions of a Janus-faced nation presented China's complex "reality" not as warranting alternating praise or condemnation but as bad and good simultaneously.

THAT FORMULATION HAS SHAPED coverage of the major China stories in the post-Tiananmen decade. The United Nations' Fourth World Conference on Women held in Beijing in September 1995, for example, not only triggered sharp criticism of Hillary Clinton's attendance from hard-liners but also occasioned a burst of articles about good women subjected to the harsh control of an unprincipled government. "Unfortunately for women," declared a September 22, 1995, editorial in the *Providence Journal-Bulletin*, "China lobbied hard to host this meeting, in hopes of improving its image after the brutal suppression of pro-democracy demonstrations in Tiananmen Square. Chinese leaders may even have had the thought that nothing could be safer and more innocuous than a women's conference. (If so, they should have thought again.)" Reports on the long-awaited death of Deng Xiaoping in February 1997 also offered juxtaposed assertions. The February 19 *Newsweek* declared the 93-year-old leader "a reformer and a despot." The February 21 *New York Post* called Deng the "architect of the 1989 Tiananmen Square student massacre" and the inspiration behind China's economic rebirth.

But it was coverage of Hong Kong's transition to Chinese rule that most consistently relied on stereotypical images and dichotomous judgments. A crescendo of media reports after 1995 described the freedom-loving colony helplessly awaiting its fate. "The signs are mounting that when China regains control of Hong Kong next July 1, Hong Kong's citizens will lose many of their freedoms," a November 21, 1996, *New York Times* editorial warned. Magazine cover stories alleged that Hong Kong was being thrown to the wolves or foresaw the end of Hong Kong. On the eve of the hand-over, a June 28 *New York Times* article cautioned—beneath the threatening headline CHINA'S ARMY IS READY FOR A DISPLAY OF FORCE—that "China's army is widely regarded with trepidation here, where memories of the suppression of pro-democracy protests at Tiananmen Square in Beijing eight years ago are still vivid.

Veteran reporter Melinda Liu explained the prevailing journalistic formulation, in the May 19, 1997 *Newsweek*, by noting that the hand-over of Hong Kong to China reversed what had come to seem the normal course of events in the modern world. "Since the late 1980s, totalitarian regimes have collapsed," she noted. And people remember "that a scant eight years ago China met the demands for the kind of freedom that Hong Kong enjoys with bullets in Tiananmen Square. After 10 years in which the bounds of liberty have been extended, it matters that 6 million people will be placed on the wrong side of the fence." Contrary to some expectations, the hand-over ceremonies, which attracted more than 8,000 reporters from abroad, proceeded without incident, and the PLA disappeared quietly into former British barracks.

Foreign media interest in Hong Kong decreased once anxiety abated that press freedom would be curtailed, demonstrations prohibited and dissidents arrested. The narrative of an innocent Hong Kong falling helpless prey to an evil Chinese dragon proved unfounded. Not only did elections in 1998 return democracy advocates to the Legislative Council, but the observance of the annual June 4 candlelight vigil proceeded without interference. China's economic intervention, once denounced as an erosion of free market capitalism, helped Hong Kong to weather the Asian financial crisis, and an influx of mainland visitors, once feared, bolstered its sagging tourist industry. The biggest threat to a reliable press in autumn 1998 was sensationalized reporting rather than Communist control.

U.S. news media emphasis on the China threat in the 1990s has drawn thoughtful comment about how, as *Newsday* wrote on June 28, 1998, "the country of current political imagination in America is not one that many Chinese, including ardent reformers, would recognize." In fact, Americans are more haunted by the memory of what happened in 1989 than the Chinese, even than student leaders like Wang Dan, Melinda Liu reported in a June 29, 1998, *Newsweek* special report on "The New China." "Nine years after the bloodshed in Beijing, which I covered for *Newsweek*, I returned to the Chinese capital to find a country racing forward, not looking back. Once a raw wound in the Chinese psyche, Tiananmen's legacy is subtler now, like a faded scar." No one who witnessed the shattering violence in 1989 can ever exorcise its ghosts, Liu stresses, but she nonetheless queries why foreigners continue to "obsess over Tiananmen" when so few Chinese share that perspective.

Indeed, many reporters recognize that while Beijing's citizens have not forgotten, they have spent nine years absorbing the tragedy and moving on, seizing new opportunities for economic advancement and personal freedom, confident that the official "verdict" on the Tiananmen events as an incidence of "counter-revolutionary turmoil" will be overturned. *Newsweek* columnist Jonathan Alter, who describes himself as formerly a "hard-line China breaker," someone "willing to smash the plates of the U.S.-China relationship," observed in the July 6, 1998, issue that "the truth is a lot more nuanced" than he had previously recognized. His views began to shift in 1997 when he covered the Hong Kong hand-over and interviewed Chinese who had fled the mainland but still believed that the Beijing leadership "would make good on its 'one China, two systems' approach." Visiting China again in 1998, Alter found a society more open than just a year before and more relaxed than he could have imagined "from all the neo-cold-war wind blowing through Washington." He acknowledges that the hard-liners' view of China as a grave military threat to the rest of Asia still sounds plausible, "especially when you see those pictures of goose-stepping soldiers. The only problem is that it's not true." Alter recommends breaking "some of our old simplistic images of China, instead of the relationship itself."

WHEN AN INFLUENTIAL COLUMNIST once hostile to Beijing argues for replacing simplistic images with nuanced observations, a shift in the media's treatment of China seems evident. But in the long and complex story of Sino-American relations, contemporary events often collide with enduring patterns. The old expectation that America can save China, if not for Christ at least for democracy, bolsters evangelism, impassioned human rights advocacy and determined commercial ventures that still attempt to convert China to the American way.

Such efforts are almost certain to collide with painful realities. Stability remains tenuous in China, and accelerating social and economic problems pose a severe challenge to the Jiang Zemin government. Financial crisis looms. Strikes, sit-ins and petitions regularly protest layoffs, crime, corruption and official malfeasance. Demonstrations and dissent, already visible in late 1998, could easily intensify. Any reprise of the violent repression seen in 1989 would prompt correspondents to draw on stock images and construct familiar stories. For all the calls for reportorial nuance in a time of constructive engagement, a return to the days of China's demonization is an enduring prospect.

Carolyn Wakeman is a professor in the Graduate School of Journalism at the University of California, Berkeley. She is the author of To the Storm: The Odyssey of a Revolutionary Chinese Woman.

8

Presidential and Scandalous

Portraits of the United States in the Chinese media

Philip J. Cunningham

ON SEPTEMBER 14, 1998, NOTHING of importance happened in the United States of America. Every news event and trend of any seriousness was unfolding in or around China, at least as far as the *People's Daily* was concerned. I put down my copy of China's flagship newspaper and took a long sip of coffee. I had traveled almost an hour by subway and on foot to buy some English newspapers in a big Western hotel, but the imported papers wouldn't arrive until after 5 p.m.

The *People's Daily* reported President Jiang Zemin praising the steely determination of the PLA troops "for their contribution to the heroic revolutionary spirit, unafraid of difficulty, bloodshed or sacrifice, in winning a complete and final victory against the floods."

Premier Zhu Rongji was also in the news; he too had just toured five provinces in the Yangzi region along China's flooded central artery. He echoed "the important words of Chairman Jiang" on the need to cultivate "flood-fighting spirit." Ditto for Vice Premier Li Ruihuan at flood sites in Manchuria and Inner Mongolia.

Looking around the hotel lobby, I found a two-day-old, dog-eared copy of the *International Herald Tribune*. battle for the presidency screamed a highlighted message above the masthead. The "World's Daily Newspaper" was crammed with stories about U.S. politics. Judging from the obsessive Clinton scandal/Starr Report coverage in the *Tribune*, America appeared to be on the verge of collapse. I thumbed through the September 14 *People's Daily* again, hoping to find something, anything about President Clinton's predicament. There was not a single article about the United States, but I did find two references to the American president. On Page 6 under International News, there was a Moscow-based report about Yeltsin, mentioning that the Russian leader had spoken to Clinton on the phone. And there was the indignant essay about Taiwan and United Nations Resolution 2758, saying that anyone who wanted to pick a fight and "oppose the One China policy would meet with sure failure. Not long ago American President Clinton had visited China and declared America's support of the Three No's policy which includes not allowing Taiwan to join the United Nations. . . . "

On the evening of September 14, CCTV news was as circumspect as the *People's Daily*, reflecting the official Communist Party line to keep the personal out of politics. It broadcast adulatory stories about the correct policies of China's leaders, the steely flood-fighting heroes and weighty international issues, such as the political crisis in Russia—but nothing on Clinton. I kept the TV on to see if "Jiaodian Fangtan" ("Focal Point"), an unusually candid news program that follows the official CCTV news, had any U.S. coverage but there was none.

That Clinton would be given the "friend of China" treatment on CCTV news did not surprise me; more people watch TV than read the newspapers, so information control is in high gear over China's airwaves. Just a few months before, Clinton's visit to China had been given polite, favorable coverage, but it did not dominate the CCTV nightly news broadcasts that focus on China in a way that is both ideological and nationalistic. The two live broadcasts of Clinton speaking in June 1998—one from Tiananmen, the other from Beijing University—gave Chinese viewers a glimpse of the American president at his best, fielding tough questions and speaking with an idealistic flourish, though the actual content of his remarks was edited out of all subsequent reports in print and television at the behest of Xinhua News Agency.

WAS AMERICAN CIVILIZATION still intact? After reading the September 14 *International Herald Tribune*, which had more than 20 stories about the Clinton scandal, I wasn't so sure. It was a sweltering, polluted, gray September evening when I set out for a cyber cafe near Beijing University to find out. Along Haidian Road, China's "Silicon Alley" and a busy thoroughfare of computer dealers and software retailers, I passed dozens of women dressed in rags carrying toddlers amid the jumble of computer cartons and illegally parked bicycles and cars. Under a billboard advertising Pingguo Diannao (Apple Computer), I was approached by a woman who interrupted nursing her child to show me a handful of pornographic video disks pulled from underneath her blouse. I chatted long enough to learn that she and the other black marketeers were migrants from impoverished Anhui Province, then brushed quickly past an aggressive line of hawkers to seek refuge in a nearby Internet cafe.

I found myself in a dimly lit room with 20 glowing computer consoles, air thick with cigarette smoke, Chinese karaoke numbers blaring from ceiling-mounted speakers. Not every one of the Chinese and Korean computers was rigged for the Internet; I could see there were computers with all banned sites appropriately blocked out in case the information police came by. I clicked onto Yahoo news while a cup of steaming coffee was placed on my mouse pad.

A few minutes later there it was, blinking before my eyes: the index for the entire Starr Report. For most Chinese, it would cost a small fortune to read on line, assuming they could read English, but it was there for the asking—the elusive information was available. I looked around to see how many of my neighbors were viewing the same. None, it turned out. Video games and e-mail were far more popular options. Nonetheless, it was heartening to see that China's information highway, while small, bumpy and littered with obstacles, has ways and byways that can get information to the people.

In the days that followed, I read the *People's Daily* and watched China's state-run television looking for news on the Starr Report and the political turmoil it was causing in the United States. My search was in vain. Then I found an explanation.

"I was here in '72 when the Watergate thing came up," said Chito Romana of ABC News, "And it was the same way then as now. Nixon was seen as a friend of China. He made a bold move to come here, so the Chinese press gave Watergate minimal coverage, even though he was up for impeachment. It was portrayed as a power struggle involving a friend of China. The same thinking is affecting the Chinese view of Clinton. He just came here, he's considered a friend, so the *People's Daily* and CCTV barely cover it. They mention votes in Congress, no details on the accusations."

Romana's three-decade perspective on China rings true. A friend of China is reluctant to criticize China, and China is reluctant to criticize friends. Even Chinese intellectuals who were quick to grumble about corruption or lack of political reform in China were surprisingly supportive of America's besieged president. "I don't get it," said a 46-year-old Communist Party official in charge of security at an international hotel. "He had a girlfriend, so what? Aren't all leaders like that?" Variations of this view were echoed everywhere I asked. "Chen Xitong was much worse," said a burly taxi driver, referring to the disgraced ex-mayor of Beijing, "We like Clinton. He showed respect when he came to China."

When Richard Nixon, another friend of China, came under fire, Communist Party publications were the only game in town. Today there's more information available, but not necessarily from the state-run press. Despite the open-door rhetoric and the startling material transformation of China's cities under economic reform, newspapers and television are still largely controlled by the Party. The Chinese press speaks with a single voice on hot-button issues such as Taiwan, Tibet and Tiananmen—deviation from the line can lead to harassment or imprisonment. On less critical issues, some diversity is tolerated, maybe even encouraged, as a way of letting off steam and experimenting with new ideas. People I spoke to in Beijing were generally well informed on the Clinton scandal. There wasn't a taxi driver who didn't know the name "Lai-wen-si-ji" (Lewinsky) and there were quite a few bawdy jokes going around as well.

THE SANCTIONED WORLDVIEW displayed in China's official press is based on axioms of Chinese political diplomacy. A positive spin is applied to allies, oblique warnings are issued to those who don't "get it," and vitriolic denunciations are lobbed at perceived enemies. In recent years, China has expressed offense at American human rights rhetoric and the talk of economic sanctions after Tiananmen, but the only issue that put the United States tentatively in the enemy slot was Taiwan, as reflected in the test shots fired over the Taiwan Straits in March 1996 as U.S. aircraft carriers headed towards the area.

In October of this year, a front-page *China Daily* article claimed that the Chinese people deeply resented the "anti-China" bills being considered in the U.S. Congress. A vicious cartoon showing a cigar-smoking, sunglass-wearing, beer-bellied ugly American delivering weapons to Taiwan appeared in *China Daily* supporting the editorial. "Any attempt to interfere in China's internal affairs is absolutely unacceptable to the Chinese side," stated Foreign Ministry spokesman Tang Guoqiang.

China is an ancient land-based empire whose military might has rarely been applied to faraway countries across the ocean, making it different from maritime imperialistic states of England, Japan and America—all of whom have a long history of intervention on other continents. As a result, China can in good faith claim to be a supporter of noninterference and noninvasion, since it restricts its hegemonic impulses to places it considers integral parts of its own territory, perceiving issues such as Taiwan and Tibet as domestic disputes.

Guo Liang, a philosopher at the Chinese Academy of Social Sciences who just published a popular book on computing, put the alleged censorship of the Starr Report in a more positive light. "It's against the principles of the Chinese government to focus too much on personal matters; the role of the official press is to deal with important political issues of the day. So it's not just a policy of ignoring Clinton's personal problems. There was also next to no coverage on Princess Diana here, even though that rocked the rest of the world."

Judged in the best possible light, Chinese official press coverage of America is highly principled, animated by several unwritten rules:

1. Don't criticize allies, whether it be Pol Pot, Kim Jong Il or Bill Clinton. Avoid the personal where possible.
2. Don't attack things that you wouldn't like others to expose about your own society, such as human rights violations, corruption of current leaders, womanizing at high levels, etc.
3. Consistently oppose policy that smacks of blatant interference in domestic affairs of other nations. The official press has been unsupportive of Nato intervention in former Yugoslavia because sanctioning foreign intervention could come back to haunt China on touchy issues like Taiwan and Tibet.

Some of the gaps in China's news coverage are based not so much on an unwillingness to inform as on an unwillingness to offend. A local publisher had a manuscript on Clinton's political troubles ready for publication on the eve of the June 1998 presidential visit to Beijing when she got a stop order from above. "Nothing critical of Clinton could be published during his visit," she said, asking that her name not be used. "Americans think the Chinese government controls the press," she explained with an ironic smile, "and because they think that, if something critical of Clinton was published at that time, the American side would mistakenly see it as a deliberate attack by the Chinese government, even though that isn't the case."

According to this line of thought, if the contents of the Starr Report were released too quickly with too much enthusiasm, it might be seen as a reflection of Chinese government thinking. And sure enough, the story came out, not in a sudden inundation like the Yangzi floods of August but like water from a leaky faucet, in drips and drabs.

China Daily, the only authorized English-language newspaper, is a mouthpiece for the ruling party, offering in English the Xinhua News Agency interpretation on all sensitive issues. *China Daily*'s monopoly on the English news market in a nation of 1.3 billion people not only instructs visitors to China about current ideology but, more importantly in the money-crazed mood of China in 1998, attracts lucrative ad money because it's got a monopoly. *China Daily* frequently runs commercial ads and foreign embassy-supplied PR pieces disguised as articles in supplement pages, but the orthodox news line is inviolable.

The September 15 *China Daily* exemplified how the official press finessed a big story critical of a friend of China: It avoided analysis, instead quoting respectable U.S. news sources with special attention to comments that put the scandal in a perspective favorable to Clinton. "U.S. POLLS SAY DON'T RESIGN—The American public hasn't caught the impeachment fever that's been sweeping the national capital. 'The media's sense of outrage is higher than the public's,' said Bill Kovach, curator of the Nieman Foundation. 'In spite of everything that people in Washington, D.C., may believe, the sun does not rise and set on Washington.'"

As the orthodox press grappled with a loud story in muted tones, the more tabloid-oriented quasi-state publications, dependent on newsstand sales, found the Lewinsky angle too much fun to ignore. *Beijing Qingnianbao* (*Beijing Youth News*), the lively voice of China's Communist Youth League, gave the first prurient glimpse of Clinton's predicament in the official Chinese press. Perhaps because it is aimed at a younger, less ideological audience, *Beijing Youth News* has a sensational shimmer, with flashy copywriting and catchy headlines. The September 14, 1998, edition offered two tidbits of news from the

United States: WHITE HOUSE LAWYERS RETORT STARR IN-
VESTIGATION REPORT AND NORTHWEST AIRLINES STRIKE
CONCLUDED. The short article about the Starr Report was supportive of Clinton. The real tickler was squirreled away in a column called
"English Green," a translation of a Reuters report that unobtrusively
broke the polite taboos of China's official press. AMERICAN PEOPLE
SPEAK OUT IN DIVERSE VOICES—As to whether or not he should
be impeached or resign, I guess as long as he can keep his pants
zipped he can stay. . . . " On September 18, *Beijing Youth News* ran
another taboo-breaking story under the guise of scientific inquiry: THE
PRESIDENTIAL DNA THAT CAN'T BE WIPED AWAY: NEITHER
DRY CLEANING NOR SOAP AND WATER. The shocker headline
grabs the reader's attention, but the article was largely technical, much
more about DNA than Clinton. The breach in good taste earned the
editor a rebuke from his superiors.

The state-run tabloid *Huanqiushibao* (*Global Times*) also "stooped"
to attract readers with a sexy Clinton cover story. Published under the
supervision of the *People's Daily*, the weekly's front page of October
11, 1998, was dominated by a striking composite photo of Hillary
Clinton smiling, looking aside, while the president, head in hand, broods
nervously. CLINTON TO FACE IMPEACHMENT CHARGES: IT'S
ONE OR THE OTHER: EITHER HE'S GOING TO RESIGN, OR
FACE SOME KIND OF PUNISHMENT. Belying the strong headline,
the *Global Times* ran a story supporting the U.S. president, saying that
his popularity had gone up despite explosive charges, that the sex
scandal was really about vicious partisan politics and that he had been
responsibly leading the country despite distraction of scandal. The
article also praised Hillary Clinton in her role as the president's No. 1
supporter and effective second president.

The down-market state publications tread where the *People's Daily*
dares not go, but no officially sanctioned publication offered the kind
of comprehensive coverage of the Starr Report that came in the October 5, 1998, issue of *Gouwu Daobao* (*Shopping Guide*). The shopping
magazine, devoted entirely to the Clinton-Lewinsky affair from cover
to cover, featured stories such as "Secrets Revealed of the Super Sex
Scandal of the Century," "Complete Accurate Text of Starr Report and
Rebuttal" and "See the Changes in American Society Through the
Clinton Sex Scandal." YELLOW PAGES, WHITE HOUSE, as the
issue was entitled, enjoyed brisk sales at curbside newsstands, usually

stacked out of view under a discreet brown paper wrap. It was officially banned by Xinhua a few days later on technical grounds—the issue was not about shopping!

IN LATE OCTOBER I'M BACK in the Internet café, which, due to some minor crackdown, has "no service today." I turn back outside to the autumn air turned chill as gale-like winds whip the dust off the streets and blow dry yellowing leaves off the stunted branches of trees lining Haidian Road. The ladies selling porno CD's are gone, replaced by a team of sun-bronzed men in sharp-looking business shirts and jackets, hawking illegal computer software, movies and pornographic video disks. The men, illegal migrants from Henan province, are more aggressive than the mother-and-child teams, and a sophisticated lookout system allows them to operate more brazenly.

Six police working in concert only delay operations for as long as it takes to scurry into an alley or doorway. Moments later the illegal vendors pop back into action as the men in uniform have just turned the corner. Every passerby, mostly Chinese students and white-collar workers, is tapped on the arm with the greeting "CD-Rom?" repeated like a bad mantra against the background of groaning traffic and screeching buses. Saying no is futile; the minute one street hustler lets you go, another takes his place, making a vaguely obscene CD-sized circle with his hands. And once they have your attention they don't like taking no for an answer.

I get about halfway down the street when I succumb to the pokes, taps, shoves and my own curiosity, asking to see what they've got. I'm hurried into a dirt-paved back alley, left, right, left to a shack with a locked door. The door opens a crack to give the latest arrival a cautious once-over, and then I'm welcomed inside and the door is closed behind me. Thousands of CDs, mostly recent films and porno offerings, are stacked in boxes and on a small table.

"Do you have anything on Clinton and Lewinsky?" I ask nervously, keeping an eye on the door.

"Of course!" The vendor of the pirated goods exclaims. "Here you go!"

I'm shown a handful of video CDs with pictures of President Clinton and the former intern. One reads: PRESIDENTIAL SEX REVEALED, the other CLINTON'S X-FILES. I don't linger to haggle over the price. I pay 10 yuan per disk and make a hasty exit. My illegal purchase from what appeared to be a well-organized criminal gang turns out to be something only a true news addict could appreciate: a four-hour compilation of Chinese-subtitled video clips of Clinton's White House testimony as pirated from UPN News on KCOP-TV of Los Angeles!

TRYING TO FOLLOW NEWS STORIES suppressed by the Beijing government makes one feel like a junkie. I started to appreciate the effect China had on my news habit, forcing me, like Chinese consumers of U.S. news, to take a cool, distant assessment of American media madness.

What's going on in America is important, but only up to a point. The tabloids will continue to rule the market for sensational sex stories and whet the appetite for more unofficial stories about the United States, filling some of the many holes left by the stratospheric official coverage. For example, the bootleg market in CDs, while mostly focused on Hollywood and Hong Kong film products, has made it possible for tens of thousands to view films critical of the Chinese government, such as documentaries about the 1989 crackdown at Tiananmen or stories on Mao's sex life.

As China's press liberalizes, with the spunky tabloids and underground publications leading the vanguard, the quality and quantity of information that is controlled or banned will most likely be reduced. Like the rickety yellow *miandi* taxis that bounce up and down Beijing's back alleys, the unofficial media may not be the ideal vehicle for the free flow of information, but they help bridge some gaps in a difficult terrain.

The down-market press may be sensational and racy, but it reflects a fondness and familiarity with things American. The large number of Chinese returning home with American college degrees also informs popular opinion on everything from the Internet revolution to fashion and architecture. The sheer volume of newspapers, entertainment magazines, CDs and videos devoted to American popular music, sports events and blockbuster films such as *Titanic* and *Saving Private Ryan* are backhanded tributes to the magnetic power of America to ordinary people in China. Even scandals are part of America's appeal. The October issue of *Nan Feng Chuang* (*Southern Wind*)
a reform-minded business monthly published in Guangzhou, ran a piece called "Scandals and Democracy" that echoed this view. "Scandals are not a bad thing. The more you hear about scandals," wrote Mr. Hu Yidao, "the more democratic the country probably is."

Two months after giving Clinton the "friend of China" treatment vis-à-vis the Starr Report, the United States was under attack for not toeing the line on Tibet and Taiwan. "The Chinese Government has expressed its serious concern and strong displeasure over these erroneous moves," said a front-page article in the November 12 *China Daily*. An editorial of the same day took a shot at America's press corps: "The Dalai Lama show is nothing but a public relations farce, despite the bluff and bluster of the Western media frenzy."

"I've seen the Chinese government swing back and forth on its assessment of America," says *Asahi Shimbun* Beijing bureau chief Kato Chihiro, "but I think one thing is clear—the Chinese people have consistently been fascinated with America. That hasn't changed and nothing the government says will make it change." If the way China looks at America is compared to the course of a great sailing ship, the vast populace on the decks remains forward-looking and even-keeled in the water, even if the government, perched way up on the masts, rocks back and forth, ordering zigzags due to changes in the wind.

Philip J. Cunningham, a 1998 Nieman fellow, is a former producer for NHK and reporter for Asahi Shimbun *and* Japan Times. *Reaching for the Sky, his account of covering the 1989 Beijing student movement, will be published on-line by 1st Books Library (spring 1999).*

9

Guiding Public Opinion

Controls and restrictions are embedded in soft-laced words.

Dai Qing

IN "MODERN" CHINA, THE PHRASE "guiding public opinion" is still heard and promulgated on the evening news and read in the papers. Despite the fact that the complex philological structure of the Chinese language often makes for a variety of interpretations to many a word and phrase, the message conveyed by this particular saying—"guiding public opinion" —is unequivocally clear and precise: "Say it this way and not that, for no other position shall be tolerated," or, better yet, "Saying it this way is to your advantage for if you insist on the opposite, well then just let's wait and see."

One could argue, of course, that "guiding public opinion" represents great progress in China, a dramatic improvement from the days of revolution and war when the common folk and intellectuals alike were ordered to abide by the Party line without question or doubt. Under the banner of "leading public opinion" "*lingdao yulan*"—one of our less valuable imports from the Leninist regime in the Soviet Union—nary a deviant word was spoken, and if so it was quickly crushed, wiped out in one fell swoop. That was more than 50 years ago, and since that time the slogan about how "the people have become the masters of the house" has been on our lips. And yet, believe it or not, it is still necessary to restrict ideas and opinions, though now with greater subtlety and nuance. Why?

73

Granted during battle and soon after a major conflict we all expect that restrictions on opinion may arise in the interest of forging national unity and dealing with remnants of the *ancien régime*. This, after all, is to be expected. With 4,000 years of civilization, China has consistently produced leaders and advisors who seem especially artful in using language to their advantage, understanding all too well that cruel and brutal rule must be glossed over with a soft veneer. And so it is in the late 1990s, when the world is witnessing the explosion information through the electronic media and the Internet, here in China controls over public opinion and publications are secured with such a seemingly innocuous phrase as "guiding public opinion." Yes, it's an improvement, but the reality of control and restriction is still embedded in its soft-laced words.

All this naturally raises the question of just how writers and journalists in China are wedded to the political pursuits of Party leaders.

ALLOW ME TO CITE A FEW EXAMPLES from past events as an illustration of how under the banner of "guiding public opinion" this control is accomplished. Whenever any potentially "newsworthy" incident (domestic or foreign) occurs, the first decision to be made by the higher-ups is whether to cover it up or have the Party issue a public announcement. Recall the great earthquake in the eastern city of Tangshan in 1976: despite the huge loss of life and devastation of local industry, the Chinese Communist Party decided to keep the scale of the disaster a secret, especially in its reports to the outside world. On other occasions, however, when floods and other natural calamities hit remote areas and prevent small children from attending school, the Party has "welcomed open coverage" in large part because it wants to attract foreign assistance to the needy.

Once coverage is allowed, then certain reporters from certain news organizations are assigned to cover the situation, though strictly in line with the "spirit" of the original decision. While some consideration is given to the professional competence of individual reporters, the more important criterion is their overall political qualification and "standpoint." Reporters sent to conduct interviews at the central leadership compound in Beijing or to a war front, for instance, must be totally trusted politically or no such assignment would be forthcoming.

Any reporter so chosen must then act with the greatest care in covering the story. Arriving at the assigned site of a disaster or major incident, the newsman begins his investigation and writing, all the while paying great heed to the intention and spin the leaders want to give to this particular story. Of equal concern is the image that the coverage presents of our sacred "motherland" and our "working people," along with the appropriate "cultivation of the Party Spirit" and the "Xinhua News Agency writing style" that all stories must fulfill. ⌉

[Last but not least, once completed, the article is subject to evaluation and inspection by three separate sections or bureaucratic organs: the reporter's own department; the office of the editor in chief; and the editor in chief or his deputy, this depending on the "importance of the article." ⌉

Whether anything resembling "news" is left in China after such treatment by this bureaucratic machine is a good question. Is it any wonder that Chinese readers constantly mock our newspapers by claiming that "the only believable story is the weather forecast?" And, should we be surprised that the common refrain about news reporters in our country is that "as individuals they're not a bad lot, but in their professional work and as a whole they are absolutely despicable"? And yet, every reader of the press in China who wants to have some idea of what's going on in the country has mastered the fine art of reading between the lines. That is, if a news article boasts that "the general situation is fabulous," then the reader figures that the real situation must be awful; if so-and-so's novel or story is bombarded with criticism, then its content and story line must be valuable and enchanting. This sounds crazy, but it's the only way to intuit our press with any intelligence.

AND THUS IT IS THAT since 1989, and especially 1995, controls over the expression of ideas and the coverage of speeches have been tightened in the Chinese press. Banned from the newsstands are not only direct criticism and candid observation of historical incidents and events across our land and the world, but even lighthearted articles aimed at provoking a bit of humor and satirical appreciation among the reading public.

Tight control over media undoubtedly makes dictators feel cozy and secure, but it is also their trap. It's easy to dismiss the sparkle of freedom and creativity against the mighty iceberg of the controlling regime, but as the warming trend of the sirocco brought on by the market economy in China gains strength, irreversibly this iceberg will slowly melt away and ultimately collapse. Doubt my words? Well, then I suggest you take a stroll by Shanghai's thriving stock market, or by the grand restaurants in Canton, or perhaps along the jewelry sellers street in Beijing's Dongdan district and, better yet, by the U.S. embassy located only a few hundred meters away from the leadership compound of Zhongnanhai, where by the hundreds vendors buy and sell their wares without one thought being given to the words and noble lines spewed out by the Ministry of Propaganda under the rubric of "guiding public opinion."

Freedom of ideas and speech is absolute and cannot be annihilated at any one juncture in history or by using any sort of alibi—for it is the most valuable spiritual wealth mankind has obtained during thousands of years of exploration. Ultimately, all who use their power to limit freedom of expression will be on the losing side of history.

Dai Qing, a 1993-94 Media Studies Center fellow, is a fellow at the Smithsonian Institute's Wilson Center. She is a former reporter for Guangming Daily. *Her article was translated by Nancy Liu and Lawrence Sullivan.*

10

Hong Kong

Still a window between China and the West

Ying Chan

EIGHTEEN MONTHS AFTER Hong Kong was returned to Chinese rule, dire predictions of the demise of press freedom in this former British colony have not materialized. The local media have remained as freewheeling and rambunctious as they were in the years leading to the handover on July 1, 1997. Hong Kong's flamboyant talk radio host, Albert Cheng, who regularly blasted Chinese officials and mishaps of the local government, was briefly silenced by a brutal attack by assailants with meat cleavers, not by the Chinese government. No arrest has been made as police continue the search for the thugs and their motives behind the ambush.

Indeed, Chinese government officials seem to have gone out of their way to adopt a hands-off policy towards Hong Kong, now known as a Special Administrative Region of China. With the SAR government taking a backseat in media matters, even the harshest critics of China concede that Chinese authorities have honored their pledge to allow Hong Kong people to enjoy various freedoms that are hallmarks of this international finance and business center. Preoccupied with economic reforms and enterprise restructuring, Beijing leaders seem to be content with leaving Hong Kong, the prime source of outside investment in China, alone.

That is the good news. The bad news is that a string of ownership changes has increased control of the local media by business interests related to mainland China, prompting speculation that Chinese authorities may try to exert control through their stakes in the local press. At the same time, threats to the viability of the Hong Kong media have surfaced from within in the form of ethical breaches, sinking credibility and loss of talents to government and private businesses. Finally, the Asian financial crisis has ushered in closings, cutbacks and layoffs at media companies.

But it is crucial that the Hong Kong media ride out the financial storm and thrive. Only a strong Hong Kong media can fully take advantage of Hong Kong's role as a window on China: a place where stories are packaged for the diaspora Chinese-language press around the world, where writers from mainland China publish their work that is banned there, and where television is produced and then broadcast to China at large. Poised between China and the outside world, Hong Kong is still playing its traditional role of a bridge that enables the Chinese to understand themselves and the rest of the world to understand China.

UNDER CHINESE LAW, REPORTERS are banned from working in China unless they have been granted permission: they must apply for the privilege each time they want to enter China to conduct reporting duties. Except for the *South China Morning Post*—the leading local English daily, owned by a Malaysian-Chinese tycoon and counted by Chinese authorities as a foreign publication—no Hong Kong media organizations are allowed to set up bureaus in China.

Yet individual Hong Kong reporters routinely travel to China for breaking news events or special projects. Many take advantage of the fact that as "compatriots" of China, native Hong Kong journalists can travel to China with a travel document issued by the official Chinese travel agency here, which is generally good for 10 years. The certificate allows its holder to enter China anytime, a provision that comes in especially handy with breaking stories when it is essential to get to the scene quickly. Native Hong Kong or Chinese reporters enjoy even easier access because they can mingle among locals without drawing unwanted attention.

The practice is not without its dangers. Xi Yang, a former reporter from *Ming Pao*, a leading local Chinese language daily, was arrested and sentenced to 12 years for publishing information on bank interest rates obtained through an acquaintance at the Peoples Bank of China. He was released in early 1997, three years into his sentence, after fellow journalists in Hong Kong and overseas mounted a spirited drive to demand his release. Other reporters have also been harassed, followed and detained.

But still, Hong Kong journalists regard the risk as part of the job and keep heading north. Through their visits, they have been able to develop a network of underground stringers throughout China—even though the practice is illegal under Chinese law. The stringers serve as eyes and ears of the Hong Kong press and even file occasional stories under pseudonyms.

Bolder dissidents who cannot publish in China send Hong Kong publications their articles. One such dissident is Bao Tong, former aide to disgraced Chinese leader Zhao Ziyang, who has remained under house arrest since he openly sided with student demonstrators shortly before the 1989 Tiananmen crackdown. Late in 1998, Bao raised eyebrows in Hong Kong when his articles commemorating political reform efforts undertaken 100 years ago appeared in *Hong Kong Economic Journal*, one of Hong Kong's most respected newspapers.

Even journalists working for U.S. media organizations, who in general observe stringent rules governing reporting activities in China, sometimes venture into China from Hong Kong when the situation demands. It is a game of hit and miss. Deborah Wang, a Hong Kong-based correspondent for ABC News, decided to go ahead when her application to visit central China, then devastated by extensive killer floods, was turned down this summer. She got her footage but was followed and harassed by no less than 15 different Chinese officials and was briefly detained at the airport.

WHEN REPORTERS STAY ON THE ground in Hong Kong, the SAR itself offers many opportunities in collecting news on China. Many Chinese businessmen, who would not speak on or off the record in China, suddenly open up once they are in Hong Kong. Frequent conferences and trade shows, attended by visitors from mainland China, help local journalists network and develop sources. TV broadcasters in particular appreciate the fact that they can easily find Hong-Kong-based commentators who would discuss Chinese affairs on camera and provide indispensable visuals. Then there is the Information Centre for Human Rights and Democratic Movement in China, which has become a major source of news on pro-democracy activities in China. With a network of informants throughout China, the Center, run by Chinese dissidents, regularly sends dispatches to the international and local media concerning the arrests of political activists in China.

Besides serving the world audience, news produced in Hong Kong also influences China. In 1993, media mogul Rupert Murdoch drew ridicule worldwide when he yanked BBC news from his satellite network, Star TV—his footprint over Asia— in a blatant move to appease the Chinese government. Now it could be the press tycoon who is having the last laugh. In a breakthrough for News Corp., Murdoch recently was received by Jiang Zemin in Beijing. While Star TV itself never made too much headway in mainland China, its fortune took a small turn in early 1996 when it teamed up with a Singapore and Hong Kong company to launch Phoenix, a Mandarin-language channel based in Hong Kong. Liu Changle, a former People's Liberation Army officer, serves as the chairman of the new satellite channel. Since then, Phoenix has gradually found its way into Chinese homes, first through satellite dishes that have been springing up all over China and more recently through the proliferation of cable networks in cities and towns. In their fierce scramble for content, local stations increasingly relay Phoenix to viewers in spite of official restrictions that limit foreign broadcasts to major hotels and compounds for senior officials. With no noticeable official efforts to enforce the ban, Phoenix is accessible, a study by a Chinese company under the Chinese Statistical Bureau found, to 36.2 million households with 140 million viewers. Independent consultants say the real reach might be lower but still sizable.

Phoenix presents low-budget programs—many of which feature friendly talking heads chatting away—and practices a lot of self-censorship. While it seems sedate by Hong Kong standards, Phoenix is making an impact in China by the mere fact of its existence. For an hour every morning, a cheerful anchorwoman reads to viewers stories selected from the day's Hong Kong newspapers as blown-up copies of the stories flash on the screen beside her. "Phoenix Express"— ("Fengwong Zaobanche") conspicuously omitting the word "news," which could be a red-flag word in China—has become a staple among many Chinese households. Two months ago, its producers were flattered when word arrived that top government officials in Beijing would like to see the program start earlier so that they can get to work on time. On January 4, 1999, Phoenix began to read newspaper stories at 7 a.m. instead of at 7:30. While officials do have access to Hong Kong papers, the Phoenix programs serve as a convenient electronic news clipping service with which to start the day. Other popular programs on Phoenix include a half-hour news program named "Current Events Express," ("Shishi Zaobanche") and news specials hosted by Taiwan-born Wu Xiaoli, who was elevated to star status when Chinese Premier Zhu Rongji openly professed to be a fan of hers earlier this year.

Phoenix's more lively format and timely news delivery is putting pressure on China Central Television, the Chinese government's main television station. When CCTV was barred by its own government to broadcast live President Clinton's arrival in Xian, his first stop in China, Phoenix delivered blanket live coverage of his entire visit with satellite uplink facilities built by CCTV in preparation for the Clinton visit. Critics noticed news shows on CCTV have been using more live shots and standups by correspondents. Its nightly newsmagazine, "Jiaodian Fangtan" ("Focal Point"), has won top ratings with its exposé of social ills and official malfeasance, though criticisms of top Party officials are still taboo.

How PHOENIX IS INCHING into China is an instructive example of how changes can come about slowly, by taking advantage of gray areas in the Chinese system. While harsh criticism of China's highhanded policies by international bodies could help, real changes will only come as locals use every available channel to engage China in the air or on the ground, pushing the limits of what's possible ever so gingerly.

Officials in Guangzhou are doing that inadvertently with the help of programming produced in Hong Kong. In China's largest southern city and an hour's train ride from Hong Kong, each state- and city-owned cable network carries five television channels from Hong Kong, including Phoenix and four others from SAR's terrestrial service, TVB and Asia TV. Here and in hundreds of towns and villages around Guangzhou, residents opt for the fast-paced Cantonese programs, both news and drama, from Hong Kong over Phoenix and indigenous Chinese channels. Hong Kong-style soap operas starring love-struck office ladies, valiant cops and quarrelsome mothers-in-law have become big hits. So are live broadcasts of election day battles for seats to the Legislative Council, Hong Kong's parliament.

There is some doctoring of the Hong Kong programs, though: news reports about exiled Chinese dissidents are blocked by color bars while local commercials replace those in the original broadcast. Still, Guangzhou residents note that incidents of censorship have grown much less frequent. Back in Hong Kong, broadcasters, who did not get any payment for the use of their programs, have launched mild protests to authorities across the border but to no avail. They can only wring their hands at the blatant piracy while taking comfort in the fact that their programs are at least bringing the outside world, with all its warts and moles, into China.

AT THE CLOSE OF 1998, THE MEDIA in Hong Kong were mired in scandals and accusations. Jimmy Lai, who has won an international reputation as a maverick publisher who dared to buck Chinese officials, printed an unprecedented front-page apology in his paper, *Apple Daily*, for having handed money "indirectly" to news sources.

Apple's admission of checkbook journalism and the public outcry against fraudulent reporting and sensationalism have revived calls for a press council, an idea raised and quickly dumped in the 1980s for fear that it could be used by Chinese authorities—then negotiating with the U.K. to regain sovereignty over Hong Kong—to control the press. Eighteen months after the handover, the public and the journalistic community have become alarmed over the media's ethical lapses—not over meddling from Beijing. A year ago, the public was apprehensive over reported self-censorship incidents at media outlets. Now the universal outcry is for more editorial self-discipline as the major papers compete for the most bloody and most gruesome pictures and tales of crime victims. The crisis has served as a reminder that while Hong Kong boasts one of the freest press in the world, the freedom could be easily eroded by the press's own bad behavior. Within the media industry, the soul-searching is continuing.

The Hong Kong media can ill afford to be small-minded, parochial or corrupt. At stake are not only the 6.6 million residents of Hong Kong or the Westerners who learn about China through the window of Hong Kong, but also the hundreds of thousands of viewers and readers in a China that is fast opening up. And at a time when U.S. media organizations are cutting back on international coverage, a well-trained and sophisticated journalistic corps in Hong Kong, well versed in the Chinese language and culture, could help inform the world about China, a country we must learn to understand and to work with.

Ying Chan, a 1997-98 Media Studies Center fellow, is a former reporter for the New York Daily News and a U.S. correspondent for Yazhou Zhoukan (Asian Weekly). *She is currently a consultant for media studies at the University of Hong Kong.*

11

Learning and Teaching

*Understand the forces of past and present and speak clearly,
even when the costs are high.*

Interview with Orville Schell

MSJ: *How did you first get interested in China?*
Orville Schell: It was a complete accident. I was at Harvard and I
wanted to take a course with my sister who was also there and gradu-
ating. The only course we could fit into our common schedule was one
that John Fairbank and Edwin Reischauer taught—a very intense course
on China, Japan and Korea. . . . Afterwards I continued on and took
more courses in history, Chinese philosophy and literature. Ultimately,
I ended up in Taiwan studying the Chinese language.

MSJ: *Was there something in Chinese and Chinese history that especially fired your imagination?*
Orville Schell: The thing that was most enticing about China at that
point—the very late '50s and early '60s—was the fact that you couldn't
go there. And that sense of inaccessibility added a tremendous aura of
mystery to China.

When I left Harvard, I spent two years in Taiwan at the National
Taiwan University, and I remember going out with friends to some
beautiful beaches facing the mainland. We had a little portable radio.
Although it was illegal, we listened to the mainland broadcast. It was

very exciting. The enigma of this forbidden place begged to be unraveled. And for someone at that stage of life, it was quite seductive.

MSJ: *You walked between the worlds of journalism and scholarship for a while, then settled on being a journalist. Why?*
Orville Schell: I really became inoculated with the bug of journalism—with writing and with working for magazines—by writing a column in *The Boston Globe* called "Our Man in Asia." So when I finished my Ph.D. orals in history at Berkeley, I decided that I just didn't want to be an academic. In 1975, I went to China and started writing pretty much full time for *The New Yorker*. But I had been deeply influenced by my academic experiences.
MSJ: *And John King Fairbank at Harvard.*
Orville Schell: Oh, yes. . . . Intellectually the way I look at China is very much a result of some of the work that Fairbank did. More than anybody I think he delineated the extreme historical sensitivity felt by China towards the West, which continues to manifest itself even now.

Understanding historically China's conception of itself—the conception of its relation to the outside world, its sense of loss of face, of self, the collapse of its own confidence, sovereignty and greatness—was very much something that came from Fairbank.

And in a funny way he was a bit of a journalist himself. He, of course, did much scholarly work but his work was also very matter of fact—no jargon, no social science mumbo jumbo. He was very much a storyteller, which is really the essence, I think, of good journalism.

MSJ: *In the mid '70s when you went to China to work in an agricultural commune and factory that led to the book In the People's Republic, what were the interests and concerns that you brought to China?*
Orville Schell: Well, it was an incredible trip because I had been trying to get to China for 15 years—it was like this phantom country. It was a bit like being a faithful Muslim and being at last allowed to make my pilgrimage to Mecca. I remember the morning I woke up— way before dawn. I so much wanted to get out on the streets, but I was completely bewildered by what I found. I was utterly unprepared in so many ways, because I thought I understood the Chinese. I spoke Chinese and had a lot of experience in Asia. I had lived in Taiwan—I had had seven Chinese roommates—for two years! I sort of knew how to get along within the culture and how to talk. However, in China, I felt

thrown off. Everything was out of whack. Of course, at that point the Americans were still viewed very much as the enemy, and mainland Chinese were so fearful of any kind of informal relationship with a Westerner.

For weeks I couldn't figure out what was wrong, why I wasn't connecting. It was a very, very chilly atmosphere. Proper, but chilly. I kept getting into trouble because I kept thinking, "Well, maybe if I just find someone and have a chance to talk alone..." Of course all of this was very menacing and threatening to someone living in Maoist China. Needless to say, the authorities who were overseeing our trip were quite alarmed at such attempts to have private discourse rather than just public ritualized discourse.

Well, I was very confused, even when I left—and I think the book, *In the People's Republic*, probably wasn't my best. But at that point everybody was confused.

On one hand, I felt a kind of admiration for China trying to do something different and going it alone—on the other hand, there was no doubt in my mind that something was hideously wrong with the place. But, at that time, I couldn't quite figure out what it was—where the discontinuity was between the rhetoric, the ideology, and the hope— the visions of the future of a more equitable place. For a Western visitor in such a carefully guarded environment, it was difficult to see the savagery that was beneath the surface in the society—the sort of mutant socialist brutality that had reduced the people to this basically inhuman state that reflected itself in such fearful coolness.

MSJ: *One of the things that came through to me in the book was that your admiration for China was strongest, it seemed, when China seemed to put itself up against trends in the West that disturbed you—consumer culture, materialism and things like that.*

Orville Schell: During the '60s and '70s, people were making all sorts of critiques of Western societies. There was a tendency to try to look elsewhere to see if there were alternative models.

So, yes, that was interesting to me. But China was not an alternative model, it turns out. In theory maybe it was, but in practice it was just an anti-model.

MSJ: *What happened to China, to your understanding of China?*

Orville Schell: I think many revolutions fail when disillusionment sets in. A sense of having been betrayed by false ideology leads people to completely banish all idealism and often even a concern for values that stress the commonweal. People then head into the most concentrated kind of self-centered, self-aggrandizing, pragmatically focused practices. And that is basically what happened in China. Of course these tendencies were augmented by the Party giving permission to people to earn money, get rich and to abandon politics.

MSJ: *Coming out of John Fairbank's classroom and the other experiences, you write with a strong sense of history. One of the things that seems to pervade your books is the sense of amnesia among many Chinese with regard to their own history. How do you talk to them as a journalist?*

Orville Schell: Often it is very hard. One of the things that I think is most lamentable about the way the Chinese Communist revolution ended is that it messed up China's sense of history so grievously that people can't even allow themselves to think about it because they have no way to make sense of it historically in an intelligent manner. The only antidote to that feeling of history having been poisoned is amnesia. Since it can't be set straight, or sometimes even discussed, it's better not to think about it. And this is very strange for a society that had for centuries so esteemed history as the great tutor. The Chinese have kind of given up now on their history, particularly in the last 50 years, because in order to investigate it, they would have to ask some questions that would be too embarrassing for the Party.

Now, most Chinese are blindly ignorant about their own history. They have had their sense of history so distorted by Party propaganda, by nationalism, by a controlled press, by an ideologically skewed curriculum in the universities, that it is really hard to have an intelligent discussion with most people—with some exceptions, of course.

MSJ: *Who?*

Orville Schell: There are some historians now who are beginning to look back at their country's historical experience—to go back before 1949 to the republican period, the dynastic period before that, without this heavy overlay of communist ideology—and to be a little bit more objective and thoughtful about it. But as a whole, I would say that in China history is a well that is still very much poisoned.

MSJ: *You once praised the photographer Marc Riboud for showing China as a universe of contrasts. Are there contrasts that you look at when you try to understand China today?*

Orville Schell: I would say that using the word 'contrasts' is a rather too elegant way of putting it. Using Mao's notion of contradictions—but contradictions that he never imagined—would be a better way to describe the situation.

China really is in a state of cognitive dissonance today in the sense that it still has the relics of its old ideology, uncancelled, floating around in a disembodied fashion over this recklessly capitalistic economy.

I mean, it is a land that in many ways is beyond being intellectually and culturally lost. It has not even gotten to the point of asking the big question of 'Who are we?' This is a very surprising state of affairs for a society that always had such a clear cultural sense of who it was—always had an orthodoxy—always had such Confucian gravity and always knew what the social hierarchy was, what orthodox values were supposed to be. And now through the serial cancellation of its former identities—of its values and sense of itself—it has really been left with nothing but the marketplace to fill in the vacuum. This country has been buffeted in this century with so many different versions of itself—it really doesn't quite know what to think or believe in.

This is true of its human relations, its marriages, its businesses and even its foreign policy. And certainly it is true for journalism. What is the ideal model of a journalist? Megaphone for the Party or free-standing independent watchdog? In China it's now a real mishmash. And no one dares to even talk about it in public because such discussion can only get one in trouble. So China just sort of muddles along with a very murky, incomplete conception of what its ideals are.

MSJ: *In trying to figure this country out in more than three decades, can you think of any mistakes that you made that you learned from in retrospect?*

Orville Schell: I am presently writing a book about Tibet, which starts back in the 17th century, with Jesuits and Capuchin Catholic missionaries who went to Lhasa to try to evangelize the Tibetans. Ever since then, we Westerners have created a whole series of imagined things that we have projected onto Tibet. They grow out of our own hopes and yearnings that have our own Western logic. The mountain climbers, military invaders, spiritualists, missionaries—each group has projected something else onto Tibet.

Now, I think in the past China also was an ink blot of a similar kind for Western projections. It is always very dangerous when people are dissatisfied in some way with their own society and have an incomplete understanding of another society. Often, because they don't know much about it or can't get there, they extrapolate or project onto it. And I think there was a measure of that certainly that went on in the '60s and '70s vis-à-vis China. And it continues on today vis-à-vis Tibet.

MSJ: *Were you part of that?*

Orville Schell: I was fascinated to know whether China could stand as an alternative, whether there was another way to do things, whether there was anything in this sort of magnificently mad end run around all the verities of Western development, Western economics, Western politics that worked. And the trip in 1975 was very important for me in the sense that it was like hitting a wall. It took a while for me to fully come to terms with what was happening—that there was actually something very dark happening in China that had nothing to do with the promise of the revolutionary theory and the hopefulness that most Chinese subscribed to when Mao came to power, namely that the old corrupt, unequal society would somehow be cleansed.

Looking back, this tendency is also a weakness of people whose intellects are young and incomplete. It is really a stage, I think, that many people go through—a stage of willingness to believe, wanting to believe, an idealism that often takes time to sort out and get a more realistic view on.

MSJ: *Can you roughly place the time of when you sorted out a new understanding of China?*

Orville Schell: It was a process. But there were moments in that 1975 trip that left me very puzzled and skeptical. I think that there are a fair number of them in the articles I did for *The New Yorker* magazine and in the subsequent book. Some of them I didn't put in the book because I was so soundly criticized—not only by some people on the trip who were just unreconstructed Stalinists, but also by the Chinese, who jumped on any visitor for any sort of errant skepticism.

There was a tremendous amount of pressure on such trips—this one had been arranged by Zhou Enlai—not to jeopardize the 'relationship' with China, or another such trip. The threat that was always hanging in the air was that if you said 'bad' things about China, or were 'unfriendly,' the Chinese would react unfavorably and cut things off.

All this was very much, I might add, a metaphor for the way in which foreign relations with China later developed and now seem to work today. The presumption is that you shouldn't criticize, you shouldn't be unfriendly, you shouldn't say anything that could be construed as nasty or the relationship will go off the rail.

This dynamic was at work then; indeed, it is always at work in China. In this way they are able to control what people write, say, think, feel—all by making the cost of truthfulness higher than what people want to pay.

MSJ: *How do you wrestle with that as a journalist when you are going to write?*

Orville Schell: I try incredibly hard to not allow myself to be blown off course. I try to say, 'Okay, here is what I think, what I understand; what I think I see, have learned, and read.' Then, I try and think through what the Chinese government's reaction will be. I try to be very clear in my mind so that these two imperatives don't become confused. And then I try to be as truthful as I can in a way that is respectful and unprovocative but that is not pandering. China has a tremendously highly evolved capacity to create panderers both among its own people and foreigners who become involved with them.

MSJ: *1999 is a year of three big anniversaries—the May 4th movement, Liberation, Tiananmen. What kind of questions do you think journalists could be drawing at this time on that anniversary?*

Orville Schell: History probably is a pretty good place to start because these are anniversaries of historical events that are like genes on the chromosome which keep expressing themselves as time passes.

When you speak of anniversaries that are not pleasant to remember, many Chinese will just say, 'Don't talk about it!' Forget the past.

But I do not belong to the school of thought that it is easier to just forget these things. And maybe in this sense I am a political Freudian: I do believe that the past is inevitably a big part of any social system and ultimately has to be dealt with—somehow.

So the reason why these anniversaries are so important is that even though people say 'Forget about them!' everybody unconsciously knows—and certainly the Party knows—they have enormous significance. That is why they are so afraid of these anniversaries. Even though they like to downplay them, they're actually very symbolic moments. And they are so important because they are moments which cause people to think and reflect. It is no accident that the Chinese have a festival, Qingming Jie, each April where they go out to visit the graves of their ancestors and sweep them clean. They want to remember their ancestors, because ancestor worship is part of a larger respect for the past.

So these anniversaries are highly symbolic moments that inevitably feed into the present. And they can have a very inflammable influence, as we saw in the 1989 anniversary of the May 4th movement. That was a potent moment.

Now, in a world where you can't speak out politically very forthrightly, Chinese are forced to deal with symbols, forced to deal in obliquity. If you can go out into the streets and demonstrate in memory of the May 4th movement in 1919 that gave rise to the Chinese Communist Party, you are on one hand seeming to respect something the Party respects. But on the other hand you are sending another message of protest, defiance and people power against the *ancien régime*. Of course, during the May 4th movement in 1919, Chinese students were demonstrating against another *ancien régime*, but everybody gets the message.

MSJ: *Have you built a special engagement with China and reporting about China into the program here at Berkeley?*
Orville Schell: Every year we have a class that ends up on a reporting trip in Hong Kong. We would like to do something in China, but it is very hard to arrange because journalism is so sensitive.

But we have had Chinese participate in a lot of our programs here. This is quite important to me. We do have a strong focus in a couple of classes on Chinese journalism and Western journalism in China.
MSJ: *It seems to me it would be very difficult to teach Chinese students in an American school of journalism, to prepare them to go to a country whose views are very different from the ones they encounter here.*
Orville Schell: Yes. Well, you are preparing people in a certain sense for friction. But I believe that it is often through friction that societies change.

There are not a lot of things that I believe in heart and soul, but one of them is a free press—even when it causes friction. I think China has suffered greatly because of the absence of press freedom there. A constrained press doesn't provide a feedback function for government, and so the alarm systems that we all depend on to warn us when things don't work don't function properly.

A controlled press makes it very difficult for them to get on top of problems, so the system isn't able to completely defend or protect itself in a healthy way.

MSJ: *When you are in a classroom teaching, what are some of the key lessons that you got from your China years that you try to teach students today?*

Orville Schell: One of the lessons that I have had to confront in China—and it is one that Americans think they normally escape but don't in fact—is the enormous pressure you always feel to tow some correct line.

In the case of China there has always been a politically correct line. In America we assume there isn't such an orthodoxy and that we are completely free to say what we want, but in actuality, there often are all sorts of pressures—whether it is the marketplace, an institution's goals or ideology, or an editor or a professor's point of view.

In China I have learned how difficult, but how important, it is to both clarify what you really think and what are the pressures being exerted on you. In other words, you must be clear about what the pressures are if you are to be truthful in what you are writing.

For many people, I think, there is real confusion between these two imperatives. And often they manifest themselves by making you want to write in a certain way, not say certain things or say them in a more positive or friendly way so as not to antagonize anyone. This dynamic is something that is definitely essential to teach students. They must know when they are taking risks, but then take them anyway.

MSJ: *Are there lessons that China has taught you?*

Orville Schell: Probably a certain skepticism. I think it was Chairman Mao who pointed out there is definitely a gap between theory and practice.

If there is anything that this century has taught us, it is the fact that you can have good theory and good intentions that end up with real limitations when they are put into practice.

China enabled itself to appear to be much that it wasn't by keeping itself isolated, keeping foreigners out so they couldn't see what was really happening. What is interesting was the fact that it wasn't just the West that couldn't see what the Revolution had turned into, but the Chinese themselves. Many Chinese, for a good 15 or 20 years after 1949, were very hopeful about Mao's Revolution.

One of the questions I always ask Chinese is: When did you begin to be really disillusioned? The key time is usually in the early '70s, after the trauma of the Cultural Revolution when people began to say, 'Well, there is something terribly wrong here.' They couldn't talk to each other openly yet, but they had begun to speak privately.

So the process of understanding the pathology of the Chinese Revolution was one that took a long time both for Chinese and foreigners to come to terms with and to understand.

One of the things that I did learn was that one really does have to be skeptical. On the other hand, as a journalist, it is, of course, very important not to write purely out of a negative attitude. I don't usually like to write about things I don't like, that I don't have some fundamental empathy or respect for. And often now that makes writing on China very difficult.

While there are some things that are quite amazing and worthy of esteem in China, there is so much about it that I find so disturbing that it is often hard to know how to come in on it in a way that doesn't seem too judgmental or prejudicial. But one must follow one's skepticism.

In many respects, if I am truthful I would have to say that in certain ways I don't find China that interesting to write about right now. I am not really interested in business per se. I was trained as a historian, and what really interests me is culture and the way societies change, in other words, China's cultural dilemma and its intellectual dilemma. And that is something that most people in China don't really care about much now, either inside China or outside China.

I think we have lost some kind of basic curiosity about culture, art, religion, psychology and history, as if none of this matters anymore. We are living in a mercantile era where business really is king, and what China has to offer now is business. So for people not interested in writing about business it is a curious moment to be looking at China. Of course, this will change, business cycles being what they are.

MSJ: *Does that account for some of the optimism in all the writing about media industries in China?*

Orville Schell: What is happening in the media in China is pretty interesting—and also a little bit depressing. What we see is enormous energy and proliferation of media outlets, but many of them reflecting a certain kind of amputated form of the media.

I don't want to make too sweeping a statement, but while there is a growing diversity in Chinese media, it is exclusive of certain kinds of key topics that are both important and interesting—subjects of a political, cultural, artistic, religious nature.

Nonetheless, the trend is hopeful. But it is almost as if China has suffered a certain kind of double jeopardy in the media—they have all the old apparatus of past
censorship in place when it comes to overt politics, but also the censorship of the marketplace has now become very powerful.

So if a story makes political trouble, a media outlet can't get advertisers because no one wants political trouble. So this weeds out a whole host of subjects. Of course we are familiar with some of that in this country, where we do not have to contend with a propaganda department's censors.

MSJ: *What does it say to you about the West that China engages with the West in recent decades and takes away from it not democracy or independent journalism but the notion of a market economy and a measure of business above all things?*

Orville Schell: Nobody would have foreseen this and the results are a great paradox. I mean, who would have thought that the Chinese Communist Party would save itself with capitalism?

Who would have thought that a kind of unalloyed market capitalism, that would make Adam Smith blush, would come to pass in China while the more democratic elements of Western governance would not?

There is a fundamental obfuscation that many people who know China primarily through their business connections make, namely that an open market equals an open society. It may help, but this presumption leads to a misapprehension both in the world of business and sometimes in Washington as well.

MSJ: *Is there a lesson to be drawn from your own work that you try to pass on to your students today?*

Orville Schell: When I first started studying China and went there, I really had a very shallow appreciation of the crucial role in society of a free press and freedom of expression, not only in a mundane way but in the way it keeps people intellectually imaginative and on their toes—keeping society and civilization vibrant. And when I see the way in which China has been culturally deadened, really lobotomized in certain crucial ways by the absence of free expression, it makes me very sad. It is an incalculable loss.

And I have really come to appreciate those people in China who stand up for a more open society, in which the press is probably the most important single element.

Had I just stayed in the United States and just been a journalist here, I would have not gained this kind of appreciation. But I have lived this in China, I have been hauled in and interrogated, I have been denied visas, and all of this has given me a much keener appreciation of a free press. I feel this understanding reverberating when I am in China, when I write, when I meet Chinese. I am always aware of the constriction on what I am supposed to say.

This is an experience that I have lived for 30 years—not like the Chinese, of course, because I didn't grow up there and I haven't been sent to a labor camp and done 19 years in prison. But just the flirtation I have had with this closed society has made me understand that freedom is very complicated. Freedom to think—not just to write what you want, but to allow the mind to become an imaginative apparatus that can think what it wants—is very precious. It is not something that comes easily in China or any totalitarian or communist society.

So I hope we can teach students here not just those distinctions between free and closed societies, but to seize that opportunity to read what they can, to think broadly, and dare to say things that are unpopular. That is their role as journalists. Their role is not to make money. Their role is not to ingratiate themselves with anyone.

Their role is to try to understand things and to speak clearly—even when the costs are high.

Orville Schell, a longtime observer of China, is dean of the Graduate School of Journalism at the University of California, Berkeley. He is most recently author of Mandate of Heaven: A New Generation of Entrepreneurs, Dissidents, Bohemians, *and* Technocrats Lays Claim to China's Future. *Robert W. Snyder interviewed him for* Media Studies Journal.

Part 3

ISSUES

The lessons of the past news coverage of China are clear. Americans need to refrain from trying to fit China into anysingle one-sentence story. —JAMES MANN

12

Framing China

*A complex country cannot be explained
with simplistic formulas.*

James Mann

ONE FINE BEIJING DAY in 1987, when I had been reporting in China for nearly three years, a "60 Minutes" crew arrived in town. They were looking to do some sort of story on China.

In his early research, the "60 Minutes" producer, Barry Lando, had come across some pieces I had written. The 10th anniversary of the death of Mao Zedong had recently passed by, and to mark the event I had done a couple of stories for *The Los Angeles Times*, pointing out that although China was in the midst of economic reforms, it remained in political terms a remarkably repressive place.

Lando was interested. He asked for the materials that had provided the basis for these stories, such as, for example, human rights reports on political prisoners like Wei Jingsheng. I was happy to oblige. When correspondent Mike Wallace arrived in town, Lando arranged a lunch, in which I tried to explain that the gee-whiz stories back in the United States about how "open" China had become bore only a vague resemblance to economic realities and none at all to politics.

Wallace looked at me dubiously. What I was saying was at odds with the images being purveyed at the time back in the United States of a happy, steadily opening China. A story about repression was clearly not the piece he had in mind.

Indeed, when that "60 Minutes" piece came out, it was like virtually every other American television and newsmagazine story of the 1980s period. It showed Chinese at discos and wearing Western clothes. The Communist Party secretary, Zhao Ziyang, was shown playing golf. As for political repression, it was nowhere to be found.

At least not then. After the Tiananmen crackdown of 1989, the idea that China was a pretty repressive place re-emerged. In fact, it came to dominate the television images of the 1990s, on "60 Minutes" and elsewhere. A Chinese-American cameraman who has lived in Beijing for decades complained a few years ago that when visiting TV correspondents arrive in China from abroad in the 1990s, they all manage to ask, in one form or another, "Take me to the repression."

I reminded him that in the broadest sense, nothing has changed. In the 1980s, visiting reporters tended to arrive at the Beijing airport with the request: "Take me to the discos and the golf courses."

THE CARDINAL SIN COMMITTED BY American news organizations in covering China is to portray it, always, in one overly simplistic frame. The American frames of China change dramatically from decade to decade, but the underlying behavior of the news organizations does not.

What do I mean by a "frame"? I mean that stories in the American media tend to be governed at any given time by a single story, image or concept. In the 1950s and the 1960s, the "frame" was of China as little blue ants or automatons. In the 1970s, following the Nixon administration's opening, the frame was of the virtuous (entertaining, cute) Chinese, displaying their timeless qualities even under communism. In the 1980s, the frame was that China was "going capitalist." And for most of the 1990s, the frame was of a repressive China.

The reduction of China to a one-dimensional frame affects coverage of China in many ways, both direct and indirect.

In the first place, the frame establishes the mindset for American visitors to China. Lacking sufficient time to see the country in any meaningful way, the visitors often fit it into their own preconceptions. One of the most famous stories about American travelers to China involves Shirley MacLaine, who visited China in the midst of Mao's Cultural Revolution and was told by a physicist that his work picking tomatoes in the countryside was as important to him as learning how to split atoms. A few years later, after Mao's death, the actress went to a state dinner in Washington and recounted this episode to Deng Xiaoping. "He lied to you," Deng told her.

Visiting journalists to China, including editors and other news executives, are as subject as was Shirley MacLaine to being misled. Time magazine editor Henry Grunwald barnstormed briefly through China in 1985 with a group of the magazine's advertisers and decreed that Deng should be named "Man of the Year." Grunewald got his way—although, in fact, 1985 was precisely the year Deng's economic reforms veered off course, leading to the political upheavals that culminated four years later with the Tiananmen Square demonstrations.

The governing frame of China also establishes the mindset of editors back home, to whom correspondents based in China report. At news desks in the United States, the natural tendency of editors and producers is to look for stories that involve, in some way, the frame.

This is not to suggest that all stories in the American press always strictly conform to whatever frame governs at a particular time. To say that would be unfair to many conscientious news organizations. Yet the frame sets the background, the assumed context, which China stories usually must deal with in one form or another. A reporter can challenge or contradict the frame but can't completely ignore it: he or she is often obliged to give at least a few paragraphs about the frame and then play off his or her story against that frame.

Thus, because the 1980s frame said that China was a steadily reforming place, then virtually any story about China needed to address in some way this image of steady reform—even if the story itself was about a different subject, like female infanticide or the decline in arable farmland.

Now, by contrast, since the American frame of the 1990s says that China is a repressive regime, then virtually every story about China seems obliged at some point to mention the theme of political repression. Thus, when the Chinese Olympic team marched in for the opening ceremonies of the 1996 Olympics in Atlanta, NBC sportscaster Bob Costas felt compelled to observe, "[O]f course, there are problems with human rights. . . ." What he said was accurate, but he was also, in effect, making a sports story about the Olympics fit into the decade's frame of China.

THE PROBLEM FOR media coverage is that China itself changes far less than do the one-dimensional American frames of it. China was vastly less open and reforming than Americans believed in the 1980s and also sometimes less repressive than the United States thought in the mid-1990s. (However, the tide seems to be turning back once again: since Bill Clinton's visit to China of June 1998, the image seems to have taken hold in America that all is well in China once again—when, in fact, there are all sorts of contrary signs of continuing represssion.)

Indeed, over time the American frames of China sometimes blatantly contradict one another. The image of dynamic change in China, which held sway in the 1980s (and, decades earlier, in Henry Luce's portrayals of Chiang Kai-shek) conflicts with the image of China as essentially changeless, which governed at the time of the Nixon opening (and, earlier, in Pearl Buck's novels).

During the late 1970s and early 1980s, it served America's Cold War interests to gloss over the darker sides of Chinese behavior. China was the United States' strategic ally against the Soviet Union, and the images in the American media helped to reinforce this relationship. The Chinese people were depicted as loyal, reliable, simple, stable, honest and trustworthy. The American stories and books of China during that era regularly passed on the following sympathetic anecdote to visitors from abroad: if you leave a used razor blade in your room at a Chinese hotel (it was said), a hotel attendant might run down the hallway to return it to you.

Now let's look at the same situation—a foreign visitor staying in a Chinese hotel—in a different decade with a different frame. In March 1994, I arrived in post-Tiananmen Beijing to accompany Secretary of State Warren Christopher on the trip where the Clinton administration was challenging China's human rights policies. On the bus ride in from the airport, a U.S. Embassy official warned the visiting American reporters, at considerable length, not to leave any sensitive documents unattended in their rooms: the Chinese hotel attendants worked for the government, he said, and they might snoop through your room while you were away.

Had Chinese hotels really been transformed, or was it only the American images, attitudes and perceptions that had changed? Presumably, some of the hotel attendants of the 1970s were working with the Chinese security apparatus and were capable of going through hotel guests' belongings.

THE SHALLOW FRAMES that color American news stories go beyond politics to economics. Read *The Economist* or the editorial pages of *The Wall Street Journal* these days, and you will find China pigeonholed into the frame of Western free-market ideology. The Chinese economy is regularly bifurcated into two simplistic categories: "thriving" private enterprises and "failing" state enterprises.

In the real-life Chinese economy, these distinctions blur. Many of the supposedly private companies bought and sold on China's stock market are not only created from state enterprises but enjoy continuing, symbiotic relationships with state enterprises.

It works like this: Sinopec, the Chinese state petroleum ministry, decides to set up a private company, Shanghai Petrochemical Co. Ltd. Out of its massive complex of state facilities in Shanghai, Sinopec takes everything that can possibly make money and puts it into the new private company, which then sells stock to raise more capital from other Chinese or foreign investors. But Sinopec—that is, the Chinese state—retains more than 60 percent, a controlling share, of the stock of the private company.

Meanwhile, all the Sinopec facilities that don't make a profit—the factory hospital, clinics, nursery and elementary school—are left in the state enterprise. Under such circumstances, can we be surprised that the state enterprise is "money-losing?" It was designed to be that way, because the state enterprises function, in effect, as China's welfare system. And should we exult that the profitability of the "private" company demonstrates the success of capitalism? The company depends on a state enterprise for its social safety net, and a majority of its shares are owned by the state.

In fact, Americans often assume the Chinese economy is more privatized than it is. When U.S. companies establish joint ventures in China, their Chinese partners are almost invariably state enterprises, not private companies. Three years ago, the American commercial officer at the U.S. Consulate in Shanghai told me he couldn't think of a single American company that had set up a joint venture with a private Chinese company.

THE LESSONS OF THE PAST NEWS coverage of China are clear. Americans need to refrain from trying to fit China into any single one-sentence story. The urge to generalize is understandable, but China is too big, too complex, too diverse to capture in a single frame.

Correspondents working inside China need to spend as much time as possible developing stories whose messages, meanings or "significance paragraphs" aren't worked out in advance. The more open-ended traveling and interviewing, the better. Unfortunately, the pressures of the job make such work ever more difficult. As China has become a more important news story, it has become harder for correspondents to leave Beijing uncovered for a few days.

Still, most China-based correspondents perform with remarkable skill. The more significant problems with framing lie elsewhere—at the headquarters of American television networks, newsmagazines and newspapers.

Producers, editors and news executives need to refrain from reducing China to a simple story. Editors and producers need to give their correspondents in China a greater range of subject matter, instead of concentrating on disco stories in one decade and tales of repression in another. And news executives should stop trying to define China on the basis of their own short-term visits there; the skill of the Chinese in entertaining and misleading foreign dignitaries is legendary.

Above all, American media coverage of China needs to challenge existing assumptions and be ready for the unexpected. By doing so, we can avoid the sense of shock that erupts in America at each swing of Chinese history, including most recently after the Tiananmen crackdown of 1989.

James Mann is foreign policy columnist for the Los Angeles Times *and the author of* About Face: A History of America's Curious Relationship with China from Nixon to Clinton *(1999) and* Beijing Jeep *(1989).*

13

Charting New Terrain

"Half the sky already has collapsed on women."

Jennifer Lin

The subject of the interview was unemployment, but the conversation shifted quickly—and inevitably—to the problems of women. Feng Lanrui, a 77-year-old economist, sipped tea as we sat in the cluttered office of her Beijing home, a pleasant refuge with a tree-shaded courtyard. I took notes as she detailed the fate of Chinese women workers as state-run factories went dark across the nation. Women were the first ones laid off, she said. They were leaned on to retire at an earlier age than their male colleagues. And once out the door, middle-aged women had fewer options in a job market that favored youth and beauty for such plentiful service jobs as store clerks or waitresses. Feng said China's millennia of feudal ways were difficult to break: society accepted that a woman could bear the loss of her job because she still had her family to tend to, whereas a man needed to play the role of bread winner. "There's a saying," Feng said, "that Chinese work units would rather hire three incapable men than one capable woman."

Half in jest, I reminded Feng of another saying, from Mao Zedong, who claimed that in his workers' paradise: "Men and women are all the same. Women can hold up half the sky." Feng needed no reminder. She was 17 years old when she ran away from home to join

Mao's troops. She was a true believer and proof of the success of women, rising to become party secretary of Beijing's Institute of Marxist-Leninist-Mao Zedong Thought. Feng shrugged off my question. "Of course, that was just a slogan," she admitted with a faint smile. "Half the sky already has collapsed on women."

As the Beijing correspondent for Knight Ridder Newspapers, I have to keep my eye on a range of topics, everything from economic reforms to matters involving the environment, education, health, foreign affairs, politics and family life. Frequently I find myself writing stories about women.

The moorings that once secured the Chinese people's lives have come undone. For many women, that has been liberating. For others, it has been unsettling. No longer are you guaranteed a job from the state, or free medical care, or even a home for your family. No longer are relationships confined by the straightjacket of Maoist morality. Divorce is common, single parenthood on the rise and adultery a popular pastime.

After 20 years of reform, new doors have opened for the ambitious. Bright college graduates can launch into lucrative business careers or travel abroad to earn their doctorates—opportunities their mothers never had. But just as many are lost in this new terrain.

What Feng said did not come as a surprise. I had been hearing similar complaints from Chinese women friends as well as from people I had met as a reporter. People like Zhu Rui, a 40-year-old unemployed Beijing textile worker who tried in vain last winter to stage a protest march on behalf of laid-off, middle-aged women like herself. Or Wang Fengxia, a chubby-faced, jobless 42-year-old mother who fretted that she was not pretty enough or thin enough to get a job as a cosmetics sales clerk in Shanghai. Or Zhai Baoqin, 38, who mops the hallways and cleans the toilets at a Beijing office building because that was the best she could do after losing her job at a state-run store. They were the characters I kept in mind as I wrote a piece in early 1998 about the problems of jobless, middle-aged women.

MANY OF THE ISSUES THAT CHINESE women are wrestling with today would be familiar to a Western audience: surviving divorce, single parenthood, mid-life career changes, day-care dilemmas. What makes the stories compelling is the contrast to the image of China from a quarter century ago: the unisex "paradise" where men and women dressed alike and were treated alike, where comrades wedded for life and never strayed. As explained by Feng, the old revolutionary, perhaps women of her generation were more liberated than young women today. Back then, poverty was a great equalizer: everyone was poor, everyone worked. But today, as the gap between the rich and poor grows wider, women seem to be left on the losing side of the equation more often than men.

Consider Wang Fengxia. I met her at a re-employment center in Shanghai last March. The biggest story in China today is the startling rise in unemployment. The government is trying to stem the losses from state enterprises by forcing them to close, cut production or lay off unnecessary workers. In Shanghai's textile industry, for example, employment in the mostly female work force has been halved. Although women make up only 39 percent of the work force in the state sector, they account for more than 60 percent of the layoffs, according to some estimates.

I traveled to Shanghai to interview the director of the re-employment center and talk to some of the clients. The Chinese media were singing the praises of job retraining—a clear tip-off that a deeper problem was lurking beneath the headline. As a rule, the state-controlled media is relentlessly upbeat. You need to read between the lines to understand what the real story is.

On the morning we met, Wang was heading to a department store to interview for a job selling cosmetics. She used to work in the day-care center of a big electronics factory. But when the children stopped coming—because the factory stopped hiring younger employees—she was told to leave. She had taken a course in how to apply makeup and another in housekeeping skills, in case she wanted to work as a hotel maid. She was optimistic—and new to the rejection of job hunting.

The next day, I caught up with her at home to see how the interview went. Not so well, as it turned out. But Wang wasn't about to give up. Neither was her 19-year-old daughter, Xue Jianjun, who also was looking for work. Petite and sweet-faced, Xue yearned to become a waitress in a fancy restaurant. She had the looks and trim figure but was terribly worried that a job would elude her because she was short. When she applied to a training school to learn waitressing skills, she wore her highest high heels because she was afraid they would reject her for being too short. She stood a little over five feet. Deng Xiaoping, I thought to myself, was even shorter than Xue, but that never stood in the way of his career.

Capitalism is new to China, raw and unfettered, and employers get away with discriminatory practices that would land a U.S. company in court. Companies can state specific height and appearance requirements for job applicants—and almost exclusively for women's jobs rather than men's. So a restaurant hiring for a waitress can set a minimum height limit of 5 feet 4 inches and require that the applicant have "pleasant features."

For all its supposed egalitarian past, China has reverted to some appallingly sexist ways. A researcher I know who used to specialize in women's issues presented a paper at an international forum on the increasing problem of sexual harassment. Her superior was furious and demanded that she write a self-criticism for publicizing such an embarrassing problem. She refused and called in sick for months—a common form of passive protest in China. Frustrated, she switched her specialty to migrant workers when she returned to the institute.

COVERING WOMEN'S ISSUES IN CHINA today has some parallels with the same beat in the United States 25 years ago. Inequality in the workplace, the changing nature of marriage, sexual harassment as well as sexual liberation: all are matters of relevance for Chinese women. In many ways, it is easier—and more fulfilling—to write about these issues.

China tightly controls the movements of foreign correspondents. In the rule book that the Chinese Foreign Ministry hands to all new foreign correspondents, journalists are required to get government permission if they want to travel outside Beijing on reporting assignments. (Technically, reporters have to seek the same approval if they want to interview anyone in Beijing as well, although no one bothers and the authorities only enforce the rule when they want to harass a reporter.) But in writing about women's issues, I can draw on what I know from sharing a cup of tea with a friend.

One of the first women I got to know after moving to China in early 1996 was Shi Jianping. I had read a short item in the newspaper about a group she was forming called the "Women's Teahouse." Shi, a divorced and remarried 41-year-old, was the ringleader. There wasn't a teahouse, just a circle of women—factory workers, a pharmacist, a doctor, a bureaucrat—bonded by the same problem: their marriages had ended. I interviewed Shi and many of the women. They invited me to a karaoke night for friends and relatives. Some of the women took the mike to pour out their sad tales of loveless marriages.

For many of them, I was the first American with whom they had ever had a conversation. They had lots of questions, many having to do with fidelity: did American wives have lots of lovers? Did everyone get divorced at least once? And the worldwide concern of couples: who does the housework? But one thing that struck me was how the women were obsessed by a novel they had all read: *Liang Ziao Yi Meng* or *The Bridges of Madison County*. They knew a dubbed version of the Meryl Streep film would be released soon, and they were dying to see it. They told me that the novel mirrored Chinese lives: giving up your true love for the sake of the family was paramount.

It gave me pause: just what was brewing in Chinese marriages? I began an informal survey, asking whomever I met whether they knew anyone who was having an affair. Turns out everyone did. But it was adultery "with Chinese characteristics." It seemed that wives—as much as husbands—thought it was OK to have an affair, so long as it didn't jeopardize the family, the core of Chinese life. It was like Francesca from *Bridges of Madison County* telling the photographer Robert Kincaid (Clint Eastwood) that she couldn't run away with him. When I went to the movie, the theater was filled with women. By the final reel, Eastwood's raspy dubbed Chinese voice was nearly drowned out by sniffling and muffled sobs.

At the same time as the *Bridges* phenomenon, the Chinese media were running gruesome reports about crimes of passion. A recurring plot was about spurned lovers throwing acid on the faces of wives/ husbands/children, disfiguring them for life. The all-time worst—and my lead for a subsequent story—was an article that ran in *Gongren Ribao* (*Workers' Daily*) about a cuckolded husband who murdered his wife's lover, chopped up his body and threw his boiled head into the sea. Chinese newspapers also ran scolding editorials about the rising divorce rate, the breakdown in traditional values and the return of modern-day concubines.

I wove it all into a trend story, tying in the fact that a committee within the National People's Congress wanted to revise the marriage law to penalize financially adulterers in the event of divorce. Wu Changzhen, a 68-year-old legal expert who was a principal drafter, told me in an interview at her home that adultery was an imported

Western social ill. No "irreconcilable differences" and a 50-50 split of assets for her—homewreckers should pay.

SOMETIMES CHINESE NEWSPAPERS actually break news and report on real trends like real media. Not surprisingly, the most aggressive newspaper in reporting the problems of women, as well as exposing social ills, is *Zhongguo Funubao* (*China Women's News*). The paper has made the problem of jobless women a priority. It pushes the envelope in airing problems that the male-dominated leadership would probably rather keep quiet. The newspaper has run hard-hitting articles about the rampant spread of prostitution, the selling of women as brides, child kidnappings and the high suicide rate of rural women.

Some of these issues reflect a culture that values the lives of sons over daughters—a situation made worse by the government's one-child rule, which has worked at thinning out the ranks of girls. And peasant families, obsessed with having a male heir, will go so far as to buy another family's son.

Occasionally there are signs that Chinese women are making progress in some areas. When a young friend set off to get her Ph.D. at Stanford, she became proof positive of the potential of women. But for every glimmer of hope, I am reminded of stories like that of little Lingling. I had heard about the toddler through a friend and traveled by plane, train and taxi to meet her family, finally hiking the final stretch on a dirt path to reach their century-old courtyard house, tucked on a lush hillside of vegetable fields and tall stands of bamboo. Sharing a bowl of sugar-filled sticky rice balls, a treat reserved for Spring Festival, the girl's parents calmly told me how they might have to give her away. The mother was pregnant with her third child. If it was a girl, the newborn would be placed with a childless neighbor. If it was a treasured boy, Lingling would go. A few months after meeting them and writing their story, I learned that the couple had another girl—a reprieve for Lingling. But there was more news—they were planning to try again.

Jennifer Lin is the Beijing correspondent for Knight Ridder Newspapers.

14

An Enormously Difficult Task

Covering business in China means trying to get hard data in a country not known for statistical reliability.

Joyce Barnathan

WHEN I INTERVIEWED ZHU RONGJI in early 1994, he thought he had his hands full as China's vice premier in charge of the economy. Intense and confident, he was fighting skyrocketing inflation, managing a torrid growth rate of 13 percent and trying to deflate huge bubbles in the property and stock markets. His job was to cool down the economy without causing too much pain. At the same time, he was angling to modernize the country's ailing banks, state enterprises and tax system. "If no big problems occur this year," he said in his un-Communist way, "I will have to thank God."

But if he thought he had a big job four years back, it's hard to imagine what he's thinking now. For Premier Zhu—and for journalists covering business in China—the story has become even more complex than it was during the go-go days of the early 1990s. Back then, China was engaged in an economic boom that suddenly converted rice fields into runways and impoverished towns into bustling industrial centers. Go to any province and you could locate any number of entrepreneurs, many of them local officials, with a rags-to-riches tale. Hardly a day passed without a headline about a multinational investing tens of millions, if not more, into what was considered the world's most promising market.

These days, all the cheap optimism is gone. China is on the brink of danger, trying to buffer itself from a financial crisis that has dragged down the rest of the region. Foreign investment isn't pouring in, and China's export machine is running into stiff regional competition. As in much of the rest of Asia, the country's banks are awash with bad debt, its state sector is a relic, and the entire system is rife with corruption. The big question now is whether China is heading into its own economic crisis. For if growth slows too much, the world's most populous nation won't be able to absorb the swelling ranks of the unemployed, setting the scene for widespread social unrest.

THE STAKES FOR CHINA ARE MUCH higher, and so are the reporting challenges. In the ever more competitive fight for global capital, China will continue to earn its share only if it reforms its antiquated economic institutions and provides greater transparency. Journalists have to determine whether China is making progress, and that means penetrating the country's banks, companies and regulatory bodies. It means trying to get hard data in a country not known for statistical reliability. And it means keeping an eye squarely on Zhu Rongji and his brain trust—not just what they say, but what they do.

IN 1994, IT WAS ENOUGH for a journalist just to keep up with China's dizzying development. I was able to interview a high-flier like the outgoing Huang Yantian, the president of Guangdong International Trust and Investment Corporation, the financial arm of the nation's wealthiest province, Guangdong. I followed the man around for a day, getting a good picture of his ambitious projects and wheeler-dealer ways. He tooled around town in a silver Lexus. He refused to allow waiters at his hotels to touch wine bottles with bare hands for fear of altering the wine's temperature. And he sent his son off to the United States for college. That made for a colorful story about this new breed of red capitalist, who had visions of starting up China's first investment bank.

Red capitalists, these days, are in disfavor. Huang, for one, is a victim of the Asia crisis, which brought to light GITIC's excesses. Japanese and Korean banks called in their loans, and Huang was no longer able to service GITIC's enormous debt. Zhu's men in Guangdong took one look at GITIC's books and sounded the alarm. Huang is also a victim of Zhu's drive to recentralize economic power and find ways to regulate a country that once was degenerating into a financial free-for-all. Zhu recently ordered that GITIC be shut down. No one in Guangdong will provide me with any details about Huang, except to say that he's under investigation.

WHILE THE CHINA BUSINESS STORY is much more complicated, access to information is greater than ever before. It's easier for a business journalist to operate in Beijing because the economy is a subject widely debated everywhere. By contrast, politics for the most part remains a taboo topic. Journalists based in Hong Kong still need to get a visa to enter the mainland, but rarely are visas held up for business journalists. As unsophisticated as the pubic relations machine in Beijing may be, officials in the foreign ministry believe they have a better chance of attracting foreign investment if they give journalists access.

Zhu is now exhorting the local press to be more aggressive in its coverage—of subjects he'd like them to address. In his drive to crack down on excesses in the provinces and put them under the grip of reform-minded regulators in Beijing, he is asking the media to spotlight how local officials are standing in the way of change. This isn't freedom of the press, but rather a Chinese version of Mikhail Gorbachev's old glasnost policy in the Soviet Union—a way to spotlight issues of importance to the leadership. But even glasnost expands the definition of what's acceptable journalism under communist rule, and it could lead journalists to test the limits more aggressively in the future, as it did in Moscow.

The Chinese press is doing a better job reporting on the business environment. The weekly newspaper *Nanfang Zhoumo* (*Southern Weekend*), one of the best publications in China, for example, will run stories, replete with good examples, that are critical of suspect business practices, policies or trends. Overall, there are more stories on how Beijing's new regulations are affecting Chinese businesses, for better or for worse. The truly official mouthpieces remain good for revealing a new government initiative or a business deal involving a state company. There might be the seeds of an interesting idea in an official publication, but the hard work is left to the reporter, who still has to determine fact from fiction.

Sources are more plentiful as well. Key sources of great economic information are the thousands of Chinese students who studied in the United States and have now returned to China to work. Many are in high positions in key ministries and regulatory agencies, working as the country's top government lawyers and bankers. Some have started up their own companies, and they provide a window into the challenges of doing business at the ground level. Still others work as top China economists for the world's leading investment banks. With their ability to speak Mandarin and penetrate the system relatively easily, their assessments are often far superior to anything you'd find in the West.

When I was reporting the collapse of GITIC, I found one such banking source who had close contacts with the company and knew the extent of its total debt. The amount was vastly more than the sums reported in the local Hong Kong press. It took a month for a story to appear in the Hong Kong papers laying out just how overextended GITIC was.

CHINA IS NO LONGER THE POLITICAL saga it was back in 1989. Back then we were asking: Could Deng Xiaoping push through reforms? Could the Communist Party survive the Tiananmen Square massacre? Did President Jiang Zemin have what it takes to be the first leader who was not old enough to have fought in the revolution? Today the China story is an economic one—of huge importance to the region and to the world. If China devalues its currency today, all bets are off that the financial crisis is soon to hit bottom. If China fails to maintain rapid annual economic growth of at least 7 percent, it risks unemployment and social unrest that could easily spill over to neighboring countries.

In these circumstances, it's more important than ever for Western business journalists to go beyond the talking heads to get into the minds of decision-makers and to sort out the good statistics from the good lies. This is an enormously difficult task. Chinese accounting standards are lax at best. Foreign auditors invited to make sense of China's corporate books so that companies can list on the stock market often find it takes months to sort out the mess. The state statistical bureau is improving its method of collecting data, but still no one takes those figures at face value. Officials claim, for example, that industrial growth is still leaping ahead, but at the same time they claim that electrical output is flagging. Experts say it's impossible to have such high output using such small amounts of energy.

There are often huge discrepancies between official statistics and those of outside experts. It's essential to get a grip on China's nonperforming loans to determine the extent of the banking crisis. China says it's only 6 percent of total loans, but others claim the figure is more like an astounding $250 billion. I use official data to determine relative progress. If the growth rate was 8 percent last year and 6 percent this year, I can see the trend and can assess the dangerous consequences of a slowdown.

Tracking down a story can also be a challenge, even if the Chinese give you access. Don't assume that once you get in the door of a company that you automatically will walk away with a blockbuster. I have met plenty of heads of Chinese companies who will sit down for an interview and then not want to provide information. They're used to the Chinese media that are generally spoon-fed what to write. It took me a frustrating 15 minutes just to get one of China's richest men to tell me how many employees worked for him. I could forget about getting anything close to his revenues or profit figures, not to mention an article.

As challenging as the job may be, the work done by U.S. business journalists is essential for global decision-makers. With so much bad data and hot air, with so many investors talking their portfolios, with so many politicians selling their party lines, it's important to have somebody without bias to winnow the wheat from the chaff. Zhu Rongji often remarks on how he leans on Alan Greenspan for advice and gives off-the-cuff critiques indicating that he also reads the Western press carefully. If he reads my publication, I want to make sure he's getting it straight.

Joyce Barnathan, a 1989-1990 Media Studies Center fellow, is Asia regional editor and Hong Kong bureau chief of Business Week.

15

Uncovering Three Gorges Dam

North American coverage of Chinese environmental issues

Wu Mei

FEBRUARY 28, 1989. BEIJING. While most Western correspondents in the city focused their attention on President George Bush's banquet with China's paramount leader Deng Xiaoping and the activities of dissident physicist Fang Lizhi, another big story was unfolding itself in the heart of the capital—yet it went virtually unnoticed by the Western press corps.

In a tree-lined courtyard near Tiananmen Square, Dai Qing, a noted journalist and writer, held an unprecedented press conference marking the publication of her book *Yangtze! Yangtze! Debate Over the Three Gorges Project*, a collection of interviews and essays that expressed serious concerns over the government's plan to build the world's largest dam on the Yangzi River. Among the hundred or so journalists who were present, only a couple of them were from Western media organizations.

The publication of the book, which was accompanied by a well-orchestrated media lobbying campaign, set off the first public challenge to Chinese government censorship of media coverage of the Three Gorges debate. *Yangtze! Yangtze!* ignited immediate debate on the Yangzi dam in the Chinese media, all amid the spring session of the National People's Congress, which was supposed to decide whether

119

to proceed with the project. Despite an order from the Central Propaganda Department that required major media organizations to use only the officially sanctioned Xinhua News Agency as a source for stories on the Three Gorges project, more than a dozen major newspapers and magazines in China—including the *People's Daily, Guangming Daily, China Daily, Workers' Daily, Wen Hui Bao, World Economic Herald, Asian-Pacific Economic Times*, and *October*—reported news of the press conference and of public opposition to the dam. Under public pressure and lobbying, the Chinese government announced in early April 1989 that it would shelve the project for the next five years. A few months later, in the wake of the bloody crackdown of Tiananmen demonstrators, the book was banned and its organizer Dai Qing was thrown into prison. The following year, the top leadership of China reached a consensus to dam the Yangzi River. Construction started in 1994 and was scheduled to finish in 2009.

Yet for all its importance, the Dai Qing press conference was barely covered by the mainstream media in North America. Except for a story in the *Christian Science Monitor*, which reported at length on Yangzi dam criticism, and a 100-word news brief in the *Los Angeles Times*, major newspapers in both the United States and Canada missed the "story." In fact, Jeanne Moore, an American then working as a free-lance journalist who co-authored an article that unveiled the behind-the-scenes story of media control and contestation of the megadam debate, had a hard time selling her article to major newspapers in America. Her story eventually appeared only in the Hong Kong-based *Asian Wall Street Journal* in March 1989. A month later a *New York Times* article on the project claimed that "the official Chinese press has covered the proposal extensively, reporting the views of both sides," but failed to mention that there had long been a government restriction on the discussion in the press and this "extensive coverage" was only the short-lived result of Dai Qing's successful launch of *Yangtze! Yangtze!*

THIS EPISODE ILLUSTRATES HOW mainstream media in North America in the 1980s responded to environment-related issues in China in general and the Three Gorges project in particular. From 1984 to 1989, when the megaproject was hotly debated in the inner circle of the Chinese government and engineering consortiums, when government agencies in both the United States and Canada were actively involved in either seeking contracts or providing feasibility studies, American coverage of the megadam was limited and, to a large extent, superficial. During this whole period, the Three Gorges dam was never a big "story" in major newspapers.

A search through the index books of The New York Times from 1984 to 1989 indicates that there were only two articles published in the period that provided information on the project. Other substantial reports in the major press included one story in *The Wall Street Journal* in 1987 and one in the *Los Angeles Times* in 1988. In comparison, due to the fact that a Canadian consortium was accepted by the Chinese government to conduct a separate feasibility study funded by the Canadian International Development Agency, the Canadian press gave relatively extensive coverage of the project. Toronto's *Globe and Mail* published, for example, more than 15 stories throughout the period—a mixture of stories about the controversy over the dam and the business opportunities it offered Canadian firms. Surprisingly enough, it covered at length the internal debate about the dam.

It was not until the early 1990s that the Yangzi dam and China's environmental problems became prominent on the agenda of major North American newsrooms. Starting in 1990, the Three Gorges dam surfaced on the agenda of the major newsrooms as one of the "hottest" issues in China. Any new development would be reported immediately by major media around the world. And in the summer of 1998, when the Yangzi Valley was threatened by the worst flooding in four decades, more than 100 news stories were carried out in a month by the Western media that made reference to the Yangzi dam project.

Patricia Adams, executive director of Probe International, a Toronto-based environmental organization that has been a leading group protesting the Three Gorges dam, said the media coverage of Three Gorges has been at an all-time high from 1994 to the present. The credit for this, however, does not belong entirely to journalists. Adams said that most of the information in the news came from the environmental community. Probe got the story from its own networks of people inside and outside China. For example, Probe received first word about the internal debate on the dam from a letter sent by Zhou Peiyuan, one of the leading dam critics in China in the mid-1980s. Dai Qing, too, was a consistent source of information. Only occasionally did the news media present information that was not already known at Probe.

Grainne Ryder, a project director with Probe International, believes that the increased coverage of the project was, to some extent, prompted by the constant campaigns of the environmental community in North America. These campaigns helped raise a great deal of public awareness of the super dam and thus created a growing demand from the public for more information. For example, more than 20 environmental groups in North America signed a letter protesting the dam in late 1988.

When Probe International started campaigning to protest against the Canadian government and corporate involvement in the megaproject in the mid-1980s, the common response it got from the government and media was that if the project had any disastrous environmental consequences, they were a Chinese problem. For Canadians, the dam meant business contracts and that was the end of the story—or so it seemed. Ryder said that it took a lot of effort on the part of Probe International and other environmental groups to push the Three Gorges issue onto the agenda of environmental concerns of the mainstream newsrooms.

In 1990, Probe International published the first book in the West, *Damming the Three Gorges: What Dam Builders Don't Want You to Know*, that chronicled the events of the Three Gorges plan and criticized the Canadian feasibility study on the dam. Four years later, it published the English version of *Yangtze! Yangtze!* These two books provided a detailed account of dissident opinions on the super hydroplant, and Probe was often quoted as representing the "other side" of views on the megadam.

However, the value of information offered by environmental activists can have its limits. Anthony Kuhn, a *Los Angeles Times* correspondent in Beijing, said that he was very careful in reporting news based on the information provided by special interests and pressure groups. He often found it biased and short of real news value.

THE THREE GORGES DAM IS ONE OF the world's most gigantic engineering projects, with the mammoth cost of more than $10 billion. According to the Chinese government, it will submerge 76,000 acres of cultivated land, dozens of cities and numerous archeological treasures, uproot 1.2 million people living in the area and threaten the habitat of a variety of endangered wildlife. The project ignited the most intensive and extensive debate in the inner circle of the Chinese government for almost 40 years. Its significance to Chinese politics, economy and society as a whole went far beyond that of a single engineering project.

The slow response of the mainstream media to the Three Gorges issue in the 1980s resulted from both external and internal constraints. The key problem was the Chinese media censorship over the project: there was very little information in the dominant news media in China until 1991. Between 1985 and 1990, the *People's Daily* carried only six articles related to the Three Gorges project. All of these were news stories reporting on the progress of various feasibility studies. It was not until late 1991 when the top-level government apparently reached a consensus on the project that the Chinese media were flooded with the propaganda campaign on the Yangzi dam. From December 1991 to April 1992, the *People's Daily* waged a three-and-half-month media campaign intended to garner support for the Three Gorges project. It ran 12 signed articles, plus a number of interviews and feature stories, all favoring the project and offered up by a techno-bureaucratic elite. However, the views of the general public were absent, and those who would be uprooted by the dam construction had almost no access to the media.

It is interesting to note that in both the North American media and the official Chinese media, the project was barely covered in the 1980s, then suddenly surfaced to the top of the agendas of major newsrooms in the early 1990s. One of the explanations for this was that foreign correspondents in Beijing had a tendency to use the content of official Chinese media such as *China Daily, People's Daily* or Xinhua News Agency as the main source for their story ideas. The practice indicated that the news agenda of foreign reporters might be influenced, to some extent, by the agenda of the official media in China. As the coverage of the Three Gorges debate was highly restricted between 1984 and 1989 due to government censorship, foreign correspondents who relied largely on these Chinese media reports had little opportunity to gauge the importance of the Yangzi project and intensiveness of the internal debate. It was only when the official media launched a massive persuasion campaign for the Three Gorges project in 1991 that the dam issue became a standard subject of the foreign press corps in Beijing.

Jan Wong, who was a Beijing correspondent for the Toronto *Globe and Mail* between the late 1980s and the mid-1990s, believes that the main problem in the coverage was that people were generally afraid to give true opinions on the project to foreign reporters. In 1991, when she interviewed people who would be relocated due to the dam, she found that at the beginning of the interview, they were all supportive. She said, "It was only when my guide, a Chinese official, told me to shut up and let him do the asking, and also to stop telling people I was a reporter, that people expressed their true opinions. They didn't want to be relocated."

Another constraint was the lack of media attention to environmental problems in China in general in the 1980s. The environmental issues of China were not a topic for the major press before the early 1990s. The limited reporting on the Three Gorges dam was usually placed in the business or science section. It was only in the 1990s that the scale and degree of environmental disasters brought about by the rapid economic development of the 1980s were gradually unveiled in the media.

The technical aspect of the Three Gorges story may be another constraint. A major part of the internal and international debate involved various specialized engineering professions and technical languages that were not only difficult to understand for the general reader, but also created obstacles for general reporters to have a thorough understanding of the whole issue.

Finally, a big story needs a dramatic effect. Throughout the 1980s, the debate of the Three Gorges was basically carried out behind closed doors. There were very few staged events like those in the 1990s, such as the big show of the National Congress assembly in 1992 that approved the project, the construction commencement ceremony in 1994 and the massive ceremony to mark the closing of the river with a cofferdam in 1997. These events gave stories a dramatic impact and made them more timely and appealing to a general public.

TODAY, REPORTING ON the Yangzi dam project is still a challenging job because the central government maintains the restriction on its criticism in the media. However, one of the sharp differences between mass media in China now and that of 15 years ago is that there is a booming market of local newspapers, commercial magazines and book publishing. There are more than 2,000 newspapers and 8,000 magazines, according to government sources, that provide a rich and alternative source of information for any journalist who is interested in covering Chinese society beyond the surface of official media. Even in the period from 1984 to 1989, a large amount of dam criticism was able to be published by the small-circulation magazine *Qunyan* (*Voice of the Masses*) associated with an intellectual and academic group. Again in this year, the disastrous flooding prompted several sharp critiques of the Three Gorges dam in local newspapers, such as the weekly newspaper *Nanfang Zhoumo* (*Southern Weekend*) in Guangzhou.

There are also indications that the censorship is developing cracks even in the official media. Last spring, a short Xinhua story surprisingly admitted that the Three Gorges construction would reduce the variety of vegetation species in the region.

Anthony Kuhn pointed out recently that although he learned plenty of news from the official Chinese media and copied story ideas from reporters of other agencies, he often got a lot of his story ideas from a variety of local press and new books. "If one digs deep enough in the Chinese press, there are always great stories that no one else in the foreign media has heard of," said Kuhn.

Another important change is the growing awareness of environmental protection among the Chinese population. A few years ago, when Jan Wong was in Beijing, she found that the Chinese did not care for the environment the way people in the West did. Now more and more ordinary citizens in China are taking actions to protect their environment. Several influential environmental NGOs have emerged in the country, such as Green Earth Volunteers and Friends of Nature, each claiming to have thousands of participants. These mounting public concerns have been accompanied and promoted by more coverage of environmental issues in the media. Environmental problems and protection have become one of the standard themes of popular media in China. Recently, *Nanfang Zhoumo* (*Southern Weekend*) launched a page devoted to environmental issues and discussions.

Kuhn agreed that the major obstacle of getting true opinions from ordinary Chinese, particularly those displaced villagers in the Three Gorges area, remains. In general, many Chinese are still very cautious about speaking to foreign reporters. But he also pointed out that there are ways to improve the practice: they all depend on whom you interview, what your topic is and how you approach the topic and your interviewee. He said that if one had personal contacts, he or she could arrange interviews fairly easily. "Generally speaking though, things are improving, officialdom is becoming more media friendly and public discourse is getting freer all the time," he concluded.

In March 1998, when the more reform-minded Zhu Rongji replaced Li Peng, who had been a strong supporter of the dam, as Chinese premier, the opposition against the dam both inside and outside China gained new momentum. In recent months, some viewpoints of veteran dam critics reappeared in the Chinese media, indicating a renewed debate within the government hierarchy. This may lead to a more concerned public questioning of the environmental impact of the Three Gorges project. Sooner or later, the Yangzi dam is bound to re-emerge as one of the crucial issues of national debate. This will create both an opportunity and a challenge for Western journalists.

Wu Mei, formerly a journalist with China Daily, *is a communications scholar and a consultant on Chinese media for business and environmental groups, including Probe International.*

16

On the Border of Visibility

Western media and the Uyghur minority

Dru C.Gladney

FEW IN THE WEST REALIZE THAT there are nearly 20 million Muslims in China and that Muslim unrest in one region, Xinjiang, has become an increasing threat to China's unity. While the situation of China's 4.6 million Tibetans and their opposition to Chinese rule has been well documented in Western media, and the Dalai Lama is frequently labeled as a "splittest" by the Xinhua News Agency, news stories about discontent in other Chinese border regions, particularly Xinjiang in northwest China, are relatively rare in the Western media. Their absence creates both a gap in Western knowledge of China and an opportunity to explore why some stories about China appear in the Western media while others do not.

The Muslim separatists of Xinjiang, in the far northwest of China, hail from a Turkic people called the Uyghur. Whatever their differences over Islam, territorial loyalties, language, politics and status, the 8 million Uyghur, who live almost entirely in Xinjiang, share a belief that their ancestors were the indigenous people of the Tarim Basin, which did not come under Chinese control until the 18th century. A 19th-century rebellion and 20th-century warlord rivalries made Chinese authority over the Uyghur uneven; they were recognized by the Chinese state in 1950 as a separate nationality, and their domain—

whose borders touch on the former Soviet nations of Central Asia and Afghanistan—was recognized as the Uyghur Autonomous Region in 1956.

The Chinese practice of "integration through immigration" has meant the in-migration of the ethnically dominant Han Chinese to the region since the 1950s, with Han populations increasing from an estimated 5 percent in 1940 to 38 percent in 1990. Like American Indians, the Uyghur have become known not as an indigenous people attached to a region once their own, but as one of 55 minority nationalities in China. Though other Muslim groups in China share some of the Uyghur complaints, none of them is as concentrated in one area with such strategic importance and natural resources. Xinjiang's vast mineral and petrochemical resources, which are processed primarily in Lanzhou and sold on the international market, further make the Uyghur and their traditional homeland important to China. (Most Uyghur claim that the funneling of profits out of the region places them at a serious economic disadvantage.) Finally, the development of the tourist industry in the region as a "Silk Road" destination follows the line of tourist development in the minority areas taking place throughout China and other developing countries.

AGAINST THIS BACKGROUND, UNREST among the Uyghur is something that the government of China takes seriously. Uyghur separatists seek to recover the land of their ancestors, today known as "Xinjiang"—which in Chinese means "new dominion," reflecting official Chinese incorporation of the region in the mid-18th century—and rename it "Eastern Turkestan," or even "Uyghuristan." Throughout the last few years, regular reports have surfaced of isolated bombings, attacks on police stations and interethnic fighting. With the March 7, 1997, bus bombings in Beijing, widely attributed (though never verified) to Uyghur Muslim separatists, coupled with the Urumqi bus bombings on the day of Deng Xiaoping's memorial on February 25, 1997, (killing nine people), Beijing began to address publicly its Muslim separatist problem. The largest uprising in the last 10 years took place February 2-7, 1997, in Yining, leaving at least 25 dead and hundreds injured and arrested. This event was, unlike other developments in Xinjiang, heavily covered by the world's news media. After denying it for decades and stressing instead China's "national unity," official Chinese reports have admitted to Muslim uprisings and "splittest" activities in its border regions.

After the February 1997 uprising, the government responded with a host of random arrests and new policy announcements. In spring 1998, the National Peoples Congress passed a new criminal law that redefined "counterrevolutionary" crimes to be "crimes against the state," liable to severe prison terms and even execution. Included in "crimes against the state" were any actions considered to involve "ethnic discrimination" or "stirring up anti-ethnic sentiment." Many human rights activists have argued that this is a thinly veiled attempt to criminalize political actions and to make them appear as illegal as traffic violations and thus support China's claims that it holds "no political prisoners." Since any minority activity could be regarded as stirring "anti-ethnic feeling," many ethnic activists are concerned that the new criminal law will be easily turned against them. At the same time, those Han Chinese—who form a majority of the people in China—who stir up ethnic problems can also be arrested.

Internationally, increasing attention is being devoted to the plight of indigenous peoples who live in border areas. Chinese authorities are correct when they note that this phenomenon has directed increased attention to China's own outlying regions. Notably, the chair of the Unrepresented Nations and People's Organization based in The Hague is Erkin Alptekin, son of the Uyghur Nationalist leader, Isa Yusuf Alptekin. And there are at least five international organizations working for the independence of Xinjiang, based in Amsterdam, Munich, Istanbul, Melbourne and Washington.

Only in the diaspora, especially among Uyghur exile communities in Turkey, Saudi Arabia, Europe and the U.S., can efforts to create an Uyghurstan proceed: efforts include frequent protests, strong participation in international organizations, such as UNPO, and a large number of Web sites and list-servs. Even with such efforts, Americans seem less than sympathetic to the Uyghur cause, and news organizations show little interest.

THE ABSENCE OF NEWS from Xinjiang in the American media is due to a combination of a lack of reporting on the ground and a lack of interest in the home offices of American news organizations. Reporters visit Xinjiang more than they used to, but their stories get killed until a bomb goes off and alerts people that there is a problem. Ultimately, it is a lack of interest, due largely to factors of politics and economics, that explains the scarcity of stories about the Uyghur. Even though the

Soviet Union broke up into 15 nations, many of them Muslim and on China's border, most analysts have argued that China will not go the way of the Soviets. China's burgeoning economy, strong military and strict border controls (monitoring not only the flow of goods and people but currency, which saved China to a major extent from the current Asian economic crisis), will, in the view of many analysts, keep the country unified for the foreseeable future. Since China's Uyghur are not a serious threat, they are not a serious news item. However, there are other reasons—cultural and economic—why the Uyghur have been largely ignored by the Western media.

Unlike Tibet, Xinjiang has never been regarded as a Shangri-la that has eluded Western penetration. Xinjiang, though isolated, has been at the crossroads of the Silk Road since Roman times, at the heart of Russia and Britain's Asian rivalry that was the "Great Game" of the 19th century. Today it is wedged among eight nations. Secondly, the Uyghur are Muslims and do not have the allure of Tibetan Buddhism to the Western elites seeking exotic alternatives to Middle Eastern and Eurocentric religious traditions. Like Chechnya and Kosovo, the Uyghur case is seen as yet one more ethnic problem among Muslims in an obscure part of the world that is of little concern to the West. Finally, the Uyghur today make up only 50 percent of the region's population, and though the region is critical to China's development, there is little that the Western powers would gain from an independent Uyghuristan. Most prefer a unified China that can purchase Western goods and provide cheap exports to a dismembered post-Soviet stepchild.

The indifference to the Uyghur that is found in the West is not, however, universal: sympathy for the Uyghur runs high in the Middle East. In the news media of Turkey, Iran, the Arab nations and the new mainly Muslim nations of Central Asia, the Uyghur cause frequently has been heralded as the plight of the "last Muslims under communism." Although the governments of Muslim nations do not officially support the Uyghur separatists, they receive wide public sympathy and Uyghur nationalist organizations proliferate. They get their message out through frequent demonstrations and graphic Web pages. Since the Uyghur speak a Turkic language and are Central Asian in culture, they receive particular sympathy from Turkey and the new Central Asian nations. And, though Muslim nations frequently disagree on just about everything, the case of Bosnia illustrates that the plight of Muslim minorities can become a rallying point and focus for financial and military support.

WHERE IS THE UYGHUR STORY GOING? Despite international Muslim sympathy, China is not threatened in the near future by the "splittests" operating inside and outside of China. China's separatists are small in number, poorly equipped, loosely linked and vastly out-gunned by the People's Liberation Army and People's Police. Local support for separatist activities, particularly in Xinjiang, is ambivalent and ambiguous at best, given the economic disparity between these regions and their foreign neighbors, which are generally much poorer and in some cases, such as Tadjikistan, riven by civil war. Memories in the region of mass starvation and widespread destruction during the Sino-Japanese and civil wars in the first half of this century, not to mention the chaotic horrors of the Cultural Revolution, are strong. China's economic progress is an important check on Uyghur secessionism: the nearby alternatives are still not that enviable. Many local activists are calling not for complete separatism or full independence but for "real autonomy," expressing concerns over environmental degradation, nuclear testing, religious freedom, overtaxation and recently imposed limits on child bearing.

Ironically, even though the dilemma of the Uyghur poses problems of the government of China, it also has its uses as
a diversion from other issues. China, by highlighting separatist threats and external intervention, can divert attention from its own domestic instabilities and natural disasters (especially flooding), economic crises (such as the Asian economic downturn's drag on China's currency), rising inflation, increased income disparity, displaced "floating populations," Hong Kong integration, Taiwan reunification and the many other internal and external problems facing Jiang Zemin's government. At the same time, a firm lid on Muslim activism in China sends a message to foreign Muslim militant organizations to stay out of China's internal affairs and to the Taliban to stay well within their Afghan borders.

In the West, it is doubtful that the Uyghur will ever become the darlings of celebrities such as Richard Gere or Harrison Ford, whose embrace of the Tibetan cause has done so much to make Tibet a prominent story in Western news media. Nevertheless, the appearance of an equivalent activist with marquee appeal in the Middle East would further bring the Uyghur case to sympathetic ears. And as more Westerners travel to Xinjiang and as China becomes increasingly dependent on its oil and mineral reserves, the case of the Uyghur will certainly become more important to Western media—but it will probably never be the subject of a feature film or television series.

Dru C. Gladney is dean of academics at the Asia-Pacific Center in Honolulu. His most recent book is Ethnic Identity in China. *The views expressed in his essay are his own and not those of the Asia-Pacific Center.*

Review Essay

Reflections of China Hands

17

From Admiration to Confrontation

Six decades of American reporting about China

Edward L. Farmer

ONLY A RELATIVE HANDFUL OF American reporters has ever been assigned to cover China. A brief survey of six of the accounts they wrote over six decades shows that they have had their hands full. War, revolution and the Cold War made access difficult; distance and cultural difference frustrated understanding. And because Chinese regimes have always been very sensitive to the way they were observed and described, they have taken great pains to manage foreign reporters. Chinese efforts to influence American reporters led to favorable coverage in the early years but to just the opposite in the post-Mao era. Consistently, American journalists have favored the underdog—leading to favorable assessments of Chinese Communists during the 1930s and 1940s, when they were rural guerrillas fighting the Japanese, and favorable assessments of Chinese democracy activists in the 1980s and 1990s who were contesting an entrenched Communist regime.

Edgar Snow's coverage of the early Communist movement, brought together in *Red Star Over China*, was the China scoop of the century. Europe was moving toward war while China was torn by civil war and Japanese encroachment. Snow's sympathies were with the underdog: he was hostile to fascism in Europe, outraged by Japanese aggression, critical of the Chinese Nationalists and enthusiastic about the Communist insurgency. He had been in China for seven years when in 1936 he leapt at the opportunity to visit the Communist-controlled territory, known formally as the Chinese People's Soviet Republic. His visit was by invitation. He knew a number of leftists in Beijing, then Peiping, including Sun Yat-sen's widow, Soong Qingling. An underground network of Communist agents provided him with a letter of introduction (written by Liu Shaoqi in invisible ink!) and contacts that allowed him safely to cross the battle lines from the Nationalist side to the Communist side.

Clearly, the initiative for Snow's trip came from the Communists. Snow was aware that the leaders of the Chinese movement wanted to get their story out and that he was their chosen instrument for doing so. His visit can be seen as part of a united-front strategy aimed at ending the bandit suppression campaigns of Chiang Kai-shek's Nationalist forces and creating unified resistance to Japan. It was also an opportune time for Mao Zedong, then consolidating his leadership position, to put an official account of his life on the record. A Chinese version of Red Star that came out before the English edition "provided countless Chinese with the first authentic information about Chinese Communists."

The most memorable part of *Red Star Over China* is Snow's biography of Mao Zedong. Mao spent many nights responding to lists of questions Snow had submitted before finally addressing the details of his personal history. The care with which the account was recorded tells us something about the emphasis Mao placed on it. Mao told his story in an artful way, describing conflicts in his family and among his schoolmates in metaphors of civil war. Aided by an interpreter, Snow recorded Mao's account in English, which was then translated back into Chinese for Mao to correct. The revised version was then retranslated into English with the aid of the official interpreter.

In a separate chapter Snow attempts his own evaluation of Mao Zedong, then 44 years old. He emphasizes a combination of native shrewdness and incisive wit with simple, even vulgar, personal habits. There was as yet no cult of the personality, and Snow rejects the notion that Mao could be the savior of China. Snow says of Mao that "he appears to be quite free from symptoms of megalomania, but he has a deep sense of personal dignity, and something about him suggests a power of ruthless decision when he deems it necessary." Snow goes on to observe that "I never saw him angry, but I heard from

others that on occasions he has been roused to an intense and wither-
ing fury. At such times his command of irony and invective is said to
be classic and lethal."

TEN YEARS AFTER EDGAR SNOW MADE his visit to "Red China," Theodore
H. White and Annalee Jacoby published their classic work, *Thunder
Out of China*—a work not so much of reporting as of instant history.
During the war years White had worked for Time, where at the insis-
tence of his boss, Henry R. Luce, his reports were routinely rewrittten
to depict Chiang Kai-shek in heroic terms. In *Thunder Out of China*,
White tried to set the record straight—earning Luce's long-term disfa-
vor.

White and Jacoby's version of the China war, published in 1946,
gives a brief and lively account of the war years laced with anecdotes,
value judgments and predictions aimed at the concerned but unin-
formed American reader. It is useful today more for what it tells us
about American attitudes and perceptions in the 1940s than it is as a
historical source on China. In this connection, White's impression of
the situation in Yenan provides an interesting contrast to what Snow
had seen a decade earlier. The cult of Mao had grown, his "personality
dominated Yenan," and he was "set on a pinnacle of adoration." Members of the political bureau would take notes on Mao's words, and
"panegyrics of the most high-flown, almost nauseatingly slavish elo-
quence" were not unusual. White notes that the Chinese rejected the
label of mere agrarian reformers and insisted that they were "Communists in the full sense of the word." Still, White emphasizes the prag-
matism and moderation of land policy during the second united front.
When he tries to make sense of Mao's wartime pronouncement on the
"New Democracy," White misses the implication that a drastic shift in
policy was in the offing. He fails to predict the land-reform campaign
that was just months away when he says: "There is little likelihood of
their returning to a policy of ruthless land confiscation or terror in the
village except under the sharpest provocation."

AMERICAN REPORTERS were not stationed in China from the founding of
the People's Republic in 1949 until the United States established diplomatic relations with Beijing in 1979. The partial exception is Edgar
Snow, who made a five-month visit to the People's Republic in 1960.
At the time, the State Department prohibited travel to China by U.S.

citizens but made exceptions for representatives of approved media organizations. Chinese policy, meanwhile, banned the entry of American journalists until such time as U.S. policy recognized Chinese sovereignty over Taiwan. Snow, who was living in Switzerland, got help on the U.S. side from his publisher, Bennett Cerf, who arranged accreditation for Snow as a representative of *Look* magazine. The Chinese simply disregarded Snow's formal credentials and admitted him as a "writer." Once in China, Snow was given access to important persons from Mao on down and subjected to an exhausting itinerary of travels personally approved by Premier Zhou Enlai.

Snow, who sets down his experiences in *The Other Side of the River*, finds himself in a new world, obliged to operate under the controlled conditions of a closed society. His transportation and lodging are arranged by the China Travel Service; officials and interpreters monitor all his interviews. He is acutely aware of the difficulty of a conspicuous foreigner having intimate conversations on sensitive subjects and the impossibility of getting to the bottom of many matters. A seasoned and skeptical observer, Snow does the best he can, relying on a combination of observations, interviews and written sources. The result is a thick report of what he saw and heard—at times critical, at times verging on the apologetic. He tries to put a positive face on matters that were traumatic for many Chinese: thought reform, the Hundred Flowers campaign, the Anti-Rightist movement and the labor camps. At one point he passes along this whopper: "A Very High Official told me quite flatly that only persons engaged in counterrevolutionary 'acts of violence' were arrested and that no mere dissenter, individualist or critic of party mistakes was punished."

Snow's visit coincided with the "three lean years" following the failure of the Great Leap Forward. His sponsors at Look asked him to find out what he could about reports of starvation in China. Snow devotes a couple of chapters to a discussion of the food supply and concludes that while there was a severe shortage of food and rationing, "there was no visible starvation and the population was in good health and working condition." We now know that in those years something like 30 million people, most of them children, died of malnutrition, one of the largest famine events in history.

While Snow was unable to see very far into domestic conditions that his hosts wished to keep hidden, he was more effective in reporting on international political issues where he could be a conduit for

Chinese views. The timing of his visit also coincided with the Sino-Soviet split, a development disbelieved and underestimated in Washington, where American assumptions of Sino-Soviet solidarity helped push Americans into deeper involvement in Vietnam. Thanks to the fame of his earlier work and his status as a person friendly to China, Snow hoped to serve as an informal channel of communication between the Chinese and American governments. Among the appendices Snow includes a detailed and nuanced interview with Zhou Enlai.

FOLLOWING PRESIDENT NIXON's historic trip to China in 1972, a number of foreign correspondents looked forward to the chance to be among the first U.S. reporters posted to Beijing. Joseph Lelyveld, now executive editor of *The New York Times*, was one such reporter. He learned Chinese and took up an assignment in Hong Kong, but the chance to open a Beijing bureau did not come on his watch. In 1979 that opportunity fell to another Times reporter, Fox Butterfield. Butterfield had graduate training in Chinese studies, had lived in Taiwan, was fluent in Chinese and had spent the last four years in Hong Kong. A great challenge lay ahead of him.

Fox Butterfield's book, *Alive in the Bitter Sea,* ushered in a new era in China reporting, a time when Americans learned a great deal more about how China worked but also a time in which reporting took on a decidedly adversarial character. Butterfield found himself living in a police state under close surveillance. His movements within the country were restricted, the servants and staff assigned to him were required to report on his activities, his telephone was tapped, and he was routinely followed. All contact with foreigners, especially reporters, was politically suspect and carefully controlled: official visits and interviews were rehearsed and participants briefed on what to say and how to act. One of the most valuable aspects of Butterfield's book is the wealth of detail he supplies about the state apparatus, the way it seeks to control Chinese lives and the price paid by those who live within the system. Butterfield focuses on the coping strategies and survival techniques developed by a resourceful people—hence the title of the book.

Despite official efforts to keep him in the dark, Butterfield's task was greatly facilitated by the fact that he was reporting during the first years of Deng Xiaoping's rule, 1979-1981. At that time Chinese were allowed, even encouraged, to denounce the excesses of the Cultural

Revolution just ended. Consequently, Butterfield found many individuals anxious to share details of the hardships and injustices they had endured. But imparting information critical of China to a foreign reporter was inherently dangerous, and Butterfield had to develop ways to meet and talk with individuals without being observed or overheard. On numerous occasions those who spoke with him were caught, interrogated, punished or even imprisoned.

Butterfield's first year in Beijing also coincided with the Democracy Wall movement in which open advocacy of democracy and human rights through speeches, posters and unofficial magazines was briefly tolerated. Deng allowed this relaxation of control to foster criticism of his predecessors and to facilitate diplomatic recognition by President Jimmy Carter, whose foreign policy stressed human rights. Before the year was over the authorities cracked down on the movement, arresting Wei Jingsheng who had brazenly criticized Deng Xiaoping's Four Modernizations by calling for a fifth: democracy. When another activist, Liu Qing, gave transcripts of Wei's trial to foreign reporters, he too was arrested and labeled a counterrevolutionary. Sympathetic coverage of these events brought the news of dissident activities to the outside world, and reports about Butterfield's stories over the Voice of America made his name known in China. Thus did a new generation of American journalists in China become conduits for the voices of protest—this time against the arbitrary rule of a Communist dictatorship.

CHINA WAKES CONSISTS OF alternating chapters by reporters Nicholas Kristof and Sheryl WuDunn who draw on their experience as a married, two-person Beijing bureau from 1988 to 1993 for *The New York Times*. For WuDunn, a third-generation Chinese-American, living in and learning about China was a personal "roots trip" in addition to a job. At times she was able to pass for a Chinese and thus go to places or buy publications routinely denied to foreigners. Her appearance was not an unmixed blessing, however, since it could lead to negative consequences, such as being fondled by a high official at a dance or being accused of aping foreigners when she wore Western clothing on the street. Her own identity questions made her sensitive to Chinese attitudes toward race and class in a number of subtle ways that enhanced her reporting.

Like other American reporters in China, Kristof and WuDunn experienced personal danger and found that obstacles were placed in their way at every turn. (Kristof tells of an American television correspondent who was so severely beaten by security agents that he was permanently disabled.) Kristof and WuDunn found their activities closely monitored by state security units. Frequent attempts were made to entrap them through telephone calls offering information or documents so they learned to be cautious with strangers. They even learned that one young Chinese man they considered a friend was a spy for state security trying to find out if they were planning to write a book. Liaison officers at the Foreign Ministry scolded them for writing stories unfavorable to China without, however, disputing their facts. After the Tiananmen Square massacre in June 1989, Kristof made strenuous efforts to determine how many people had been killed and where, in relation to Tiananmen, they had died. The official response was to denounce Kristof by name in the *People's Daily* and on television as one who "has in his reports boldly made false assumptions, played games with numbers and spread new lies."

Difficult as reporting on China was for foreign reporters, the real cost was to Chinese informants:

> The problem with the surveillance is not, of course, just that it robs us of our privacy. We got used to the idea that our bedroom was bugged. We didn't protest when the Foreign Ministry ordered the tax bureau to give us trouble, when State Security burglarized our office, when police stole our car license plates, when the post office confiscated our mail, when agents scraped the paint off three sides of our car so that they could recognize it more easily. The real problem was the risk

to our friends, acquaintances, and sources. In at least eighteen cases since China launched its open-door policy in 1978, Chinese have gone to prison or labor camp for terms of up to life imprisonment because they helped foreign correspondents.

It is fortunate that Kristof and WuDunn stayed as long as they did. They came to China after language study in Taiwan and work experience in Hong Kong, just married, and full of enthusiasm for things Chinese. The June 1989 massacre left them deeply shaken. Had they written a book about China shortly after that event, when Americans could not think of China in any terms but the massacre of students and the suppression of human rights, they might well have painted an entirely negative picture. Had they done so they would have missed the next chapter in the story—how China returned to the business of development. *China Wakes* is intended to be a balanced portrait of both the repressive savagery of the regime and the growing power unleashed by Deng Xiaoping's second revolution. Nevertheless, the anecdotes and stories Kristof and WuDunn weave throughout their account are so moving, reveal so many problems and so much moral degradation, that the reader comes away with an overall negative impression.

ORVILLE SCHELL'S *MANDATE OF Heaven* is more successful than *China Wakes* in making the transition from the events of 1989 to the new conditions of the early 1990s. Schell has written a chronological account in five parts, starting with the student movement in Tiananmen Square and its suppression, the flight of the participants and the aftermath. The last two parts describe cultural change and the economic boom.

Schell is unabashedly on the side of the student demonstrators and critics of the dictatorship. His acquaintance with leading intellectual dissidents and sympathy for their cause pushes his reporting along the spectrum toward advocacy. When in 1961 the Public Security Bureau learned that he was vice chair of Asia Watch, they banned a talk on "The Silence of Chinese Intellectuals" that Schell was scheduled to give at the Beijing Foreign Correspondent's Club. The way news of the cancellation made contact with him a liability for his Chinese friends led Schell to an insight about the silence of the intellectuals:

> Once an individual is tainted by accusation, he becomes ensnared in a crippling psychological paradox. Not only is he made to feel sullied, but at the same time he also acquires the unshakable capacity to sully everyone he comes in contact with as well. Thus in one deft stroke, the Party is able to contrive a devastating condition of double jeopardy. First, it cripples those it condemns with accusations of political incorrectness, and then it delivers a coup de grace by transforming the accused from simple victims into potential destroyers of all their friends and relatives as well.

So what has changed from *Red Star Over China* to the *Mandate of Heaven?* It is not just that the Chinese Communist Party has evolved from a virtuous rural insurgency to an oppressive entrenched dictatorship. The Party was always harshly oppressive to intellectuals; it is the understanding of American reporters that has changed. The more they have learned about the cruelty of the Communist system, the more they have tried to expose it; and the more they have tried to expose it, the more the system has turned on them. Ironically, the effort of reporters to tell China's secrets has made them dangerous to the very people they seek to help.

Edward L. Farmer is a professor of history at the University of Minnesota, Minneapolis, and author of Zhu Yuanzhang and Early Ming Legislation: The Reordering of Chinese Society Following the Era of Mongol Rule.

For Further Reading

Covering China

Bishop, Robert L. *Qi Lai! Mobilizing One Billion Chinese: The Chinese Communication System.* Ames, Iowa: Iowa State University Press, 1989.

Chang, Tsan-Kuo. *The Press and China Policy: The Illusion of Sino-American Relations, 1950-1984.* Norwood, N.J.: Ablex Publishing Corporation, 1993.

Chang, Won Ho. *Mass Media in China: The History and the Future.* Ames, Iowa: Iowa State University Press, 1989.

Chinoy, Mike. *China Live: Two Decades in the Heart of the Dragon.* Atlanta: Turner Publishing, Inc., 1997.

Chu, Godwin C., and Yanan Ju. *The Great Wall in Ruins: Communication and Cultural Change in China.* Albany, N.Y.: State University of New York Press, 1993.

Conn, Peter. *Pearl S. Buck: A Cultural Biography.* New York: Cambridge University Press, 1996.

Fairbank, John. *The United States and China.* Cambridge, Mass.: Harvard University Press, 1983 (4th edition).

Gladney, Dru C. *Ethnic Identity in China: The Making of a Muslim Minority Nationality.* Fort Worth, Texas: Harcourt Brace College Publishers, 1998.

Jernow, Allison Liu. *"Don't Force Us to Lie": The Struggle of Chinese Journalists in the Reform Era.* New York: Committee to Protect Journalists, 1993.

Lee, Chin-Chuan, ed. *Voices of China: The Interplay of Politics and Journalism.* New York: The Guilford Press, 1990.

Liu, Binyan. *A Higher Kind of Loyalty: A Memoir by China's Foremost Journalist.* New York: Pantheon Books, 1990.

Liu, Melinda, Peter Turnley, and David Turnley. *Beijing Spring.* New York: Stewart, Tabori & Chang, 1989.

MacKinnon, Stephen, and Janice R. MacKinnon. *Agnes Smedley: The Life and Times of an American Radical.* Berkeley, Calif.: University of California Press, 1988.

MacKinnon, Stephen, and Oris Friesen. *China Reporting: An Oral History of American Journalism in the 1930s and 1940s.* Berkeley, Calif.: University of California Press, 1987.

Mann, James. *About Face: A History of America's Curious Relationship with China from Nixon to Clinton.* New York: Alfred A. Knopf, 1999.

Nathan, Andrew J., and Robert S. Ross. *The Great Wall and the Empty Fortress: China's Search for Security.* New York: W.W. Norton & Company, 1998.

Porter, Robin, ed. *Reporting the News from China.* London: Royal Institute of International Affairs, 1992.

Qing, Dai. *The River Dragon Has Come! The Three Gorges Dam and the Fate of China's Yangtze River and Its People.* Armonk, N.Y.: M.E. Sharpe, 1998.

____. *Yangtze! Yangtze! Debate Over the Three Gorges Project.* London: Earthscan Publications, 1994.

Rand, Peter. *China Hands: The Adventures and Ordeals of the American Journalists Who Joined Forces with the Great Chinese Revolution.* New York: Simon & Schuster, 1995.

Schell, Orville. *Mandate of Heaven: A New Generation of Entrepreneurs, Dissidents, Bohemians, and Technocrats Lays Claim to China's Future.* New York: Simon & Schuster, 1994.

____. *In the People's Republic: An American's First-Hand View of Living and Working in China.* New York: Random House, 1977.

Spence, Jonathan D. *The Chan's Great Continent: China in Western Minds.* New York: W.W. Norton & Co., 1998.

____. *The Search for Modern China.* New York: W. W. Norton & Co., 1990.

Topping, Audrey. *The Splendors of Tibet.* New York, N.Y.: SINO Pub. & Co., 1980.

____. *Dawn Wakes in the East.* New York: Harper & Row, 1973.

Topping, Seymour. *Journey Between Two Chinas.* New York: Harper & Row, 1972.

Topping, Seymour, Tillman Durdin, and James Reston. *The New York Times Report from Red China.* New York: Quadrangle Books, 1971.

Wasserstrom, Jeffrey. *Putting 1989 in Historical Perspective: Pitfalls and Possibilities.* Durham, N.C.: Asian/Pacific Studies Institute, Duke University Press, 1993.

Wasserstrom, Jeffrey, and Elizabeth Perry, ed. *Popular Protest and Political Culture in Modern China: Learning from 1989.* Boulder, Colo.: Westview Press, 1992.

Wakeman, Carolyn, and Yue Daiyun. *To the Storm: The Odyssey of a Revolutionary Chinese Woman.* Berkeley: University of California Press, 1985.

Zha, Jianying. *China Pop: How Soap Operas, Tabloids, and Bestsellers are Transforming a Culture.* New York: The New Press, 1995.

Zhao, Yeuzhi. *Media, Market and Democracy in China: Between the Party Line and the Bottom Line.* Urbana, Ill.: University of Illinois Press, 1998.

Subject Index